TURKISH BAKERY
Delight

Deniz Göktürk Akçakanat

NH
NEW
HOLLAND

I dedicate this book to my lovely daughter,
Shaman

Contents

Introduction

I wrote this book because I wanted to share with readers my lifelong passion for Turkish baking and desserts.

My interest goes back to my childhood. I remember crying to my mother to buy me the traditional flour cookies, 'un kurabiyesi', while passing in front of each and every bakery shop in Istanbul. Every time I walked into a bakery I never wanted to leave because of the incredible products I saw and the delicious, tasty smell inside.

I also recall going to a bakery shop every day during my school years, even in remote areas, to buy and eat different desserts. I must admit that my diet then was made up of sweet and savory products, aided by my mother who made the finest selection of Turkish desserts.

As a child I had the perfect mother. When I was little she wanted me to help her every time she prepared food in the kitchen. She was also talented at making handicrafts and I believe I gained my vision and my patience through helping her at home.

In later years, playing with the recipes provided me with the ability to combine ingredients in new ways and create different results from the processes.

I believe that cooking is one of the most difficult professions in the world, yet the most passionate. It is the ultimate chemistry—every ingredient that comes together initiates a different reaction; the result is either positive or negative. There is no way to change a negative result to a positive one. You can only learn your lesson from the results. In this profession, progress requires a great deal of patience and passion.

To me, nothing is more fulfilling then preparing and finishing a dessert. During a test, a product should achieve a balance of perfect chemistry and taste, and it should work for all my senses. Only then is a product finished, and I have only put these successful recipes in this book.

Turkish desserts have always had a special place in my life. All the important days and surprises in my life were coloured by a dessert. The unforgettable memories of my childhood are the times that I spent in our big kitchen with family and friends; and almost all of these moments were sweetened by some traditional Turkish dessert. After childhood, sweets and desserts became my profession and my passion. It is an adventure of chemistry and ingredients that keeps me working for hours with love.

Turkish cuisine, the food of the Ottoman Empire, is one of the richest and most diverse in the world. When the first Turkish pioneers moved into Anatolia in the 11th century, they brought with them their own customs, culture and food from the semi-nomadic lifestyle on the Asian steppes. Through centuries these were blended with the customs, culture and food of the original settlers of Anatolia and with those of all the other lands the Turks kept on invading relentlessly for another 500 years.

Turks have given the world Turkish 'coffee', 'delight', 'bread', 'kebabs' and 'yogurt' (originally a Turkish word and invention). However, not many readers would have experienced the lesser-known art of Turkish baked goods and desserts.

Located on the crossroads between Europe, Asia and Africa, Turkey is a thoroughfare of trade routes. The Turkish people have always been blessed with easy access to a wide variety of exotic produce and ingredients, as well as recipes and cooking styles. Being a prosperous community, food was regarded as an enjoyment rather than just a necessity. This resulted in the development of a wide variety of delicious recipes and naturally a lot of 'indulgence' food. One of the most memorable legacies of the Ottoman Empire on modern Turkish cuisine has been the ultimate dining experience prepared in the palace kitchen, for the Sultan, his officials and his large 'family'.

At its height, the Ottoman Empire reigned over 20 countries in South-Eastern Europe, the Middle East and North Africa. The empire's kitchen served the palace with the chefs and masters of three continents for nearly 500 years. By the 17th century, about 1300 kitchen staff personnel were housed in the palace full time. The cooks specialised in hundreds of different dishes of vast regional variety and would feed as many as 10,000 palace staff a day. Trays of food were distributed to the ordinary city dwellers as a royal gift. The power and prosperity of the Ottoman rule was reflected in the style of food and recipes, as well as the rich and elegant art and culture of the era.

Today, this art and tradition is still alive in the Turkish family kitchen, being enjoyed by the great-grand children of the masters of the art. Unique and elaborate recipes are very well preserved and available commercially today; patisseries, specialty dessert shops and restaurants specialising in authentic regional food offer excellent examples of this tradition. Many of these centuries-old family establishments produce and sell traditional Turkish sweets, desserts or pastries nationally and internationally.

Hospitality is firmly embedded in the Turkish tradition and guests are always offered generous servings of food. If you are invited to a Turkish home between meals, say, for 'afternoon tea' make sure you do not have lunch! Going by the Turkish adage 'Let's eat sweet and talk sweet', you will be offered an array of pastries, cakes, and cookies with your tea, which will get topped up endlessly, possibly followed by Turkish coffee and desserts. You will not need dinner that day. If you are invited for dinner…well, just take this advice and skip afternoon tea.

Turkish families have close relationships with the relatives, friends and neighbours who frequently prepare, eat and share their desserts and pastries. Housewives organise gatherings amongst themselves on a rotating basis; one such occasion is called 'gün', meaning 'day', where a vast variety of food is offered to guests, who also bring over their own creations. I remember coming back from school to a house full of ladies, chat, laughter and an irresistible aroma of freshly baked cakes and pastries. The food was so tempting and delicious, I actually decided that was what I wanted to do in the future!

Turkish baking and pastry has its roots in the regional and rural lifestyle and some recipes were perfected and brought to fame by the palace kitchen. The traditional recipes and cooking styles were developed and have been enriched with European styles and products with different interpretations over the years. In this book, I have introduced a mixture of traditional cooking, some with a contemporary European touch and some with my own!

Turkish baking becomes an art as it involves preparation of different desserts and dough with creative ingredients and fillings. Syrupy desserts, milky desserts or böreks (Turkish pastries with various ingredients and shapes)—all categories have their own character and taste, and some are connected with different occasions.

Black cumin seeds, sesame seeds, walnuts, pistachio, cheese and cinnamon are common ingredients used all through Turkish baked goods and desserts. Unusual or exotic ingredients are also used all through this tradition. I am sure the reader will find some recipes very rewarding for the novel taste experience.

The book includes a wide variety of dough and application methods and I hope it will inspire chefs, culinary students and anyone who enjoys cooking. I have included a diverse range of products (some of which may come as a surprise) for those who wish to experiment and explore. I have chosen recipes that are relatively simple and open to creative interpretation.

Names of some dishes are almost impossible to translate, so I have included the original names of the recipes in italics with their Turkish spelling. A basic guide to Turkish pronunciation and a glossary of terms, names and ingredients will be of help to readers who wish to find out a little bit more.

Afiyet olsun!
(Enjoy!)

Deniz

Breads
& Tasty Treats

Breakfast Buns with Ricotta

Poğaça

Crisp on the outside, soft on the inside; this is a popular fast breakfast for many Turks!

Makes 8

Ingredients

2 cups plain (all-purpose) flour

1¾ teaspoons salt

3 teaspoons sugar

2 teaspoons dry yeast

1 egg

½ cup warm water

125 g (4 oz) butter

200 g (7 oz) ricotta cheese

sesame seeds

black sesame seeds

1 egg, beaten, for egg wash

olive oil

Method

Preheat oven to 70°C (150°F/Gas Mark 1/4).

Place flour, salt and sugar in a mixing bowl and make a well in the centre. Mix the yeast with 2 teaspoons of extra water in the well. Add egg and warm water, mixing slowly. Knead into a soft dough.

The dough should be of a sticky-soft consistency. Sift a little flour over the dough then form it into a ball and leave to rest for 15 minutes.

Divide the dough into 8 equal pieces. Brush your palms with oil and roll each piece into a ball. If the balls are still too sticky, sprinkle with a little flour. Using your fingers, stretch each ball out into a flat circle on an oily surface. Divide the butter into 8 equal pieces. Place a piece of butter in the middle of each piece of dough. Fold the dough up and inwards on the butter and stretch the dough out flat again. Add a tablespoon of ricotta cheese in the middle of the piece of dough and roll again to get a good ball shape. Place the balls on a non-stick baking tray brushed with oil, leaving 4 cm (1½ in) of space around each ball.

Place the tray in the oven, with the door open, for 20 minutes. The balls will double in size after proofing. Remove tray from oven and turn oven heat up to 200°C (400°F/Gas Mark 6).

Brush egg wash on top of the buns, then sprinkle a mix of sesame seeds over the buns. Bake 20–25 minutes until buns are golden brown. These taste best when served warm.

Olive Rolls

Zeytinli Açma

These rolls are one of the traditional breakfast meals in Turkey and you can choose from plain, cheese or with olive, like this recipe. They make a very good breakfast with feta cheese and Turkish tea (see page 151). Nigella (black cumin) seeds are a popular decoration for Turkish breads; they are delicious and have many healing properties.

Makes 4

Ingredients

200 g (7 oz) pitted olives
500 g (1 lb) flour
15 g (½ oz) salt
15 g (½ oz) dry yeast
25 g (1 oz) sugar
1 egg
50 g (2 oz) butter
300 ml (10 fl oz) warm
  water
150 g (5 oz) extra butter
nigella (black cumin) seeds
olive oil

Method

Preheat oven to 70°C (150°F/Gas Mark ¼). Puree pitted olives in a kitchen processor.

Place flour and salt in a mixing bowl, and make a well in the centre. Mix the yeast with 2 teaspoons of extra water in the well. Add sugar, egg and butter. Pour in warm water and combine ingredients until you have a smooth, soft dough. Allow the dough to rest for 30 minutes in a bowl, covered with a tea towel.

Cut the dough and extra butter into 4 equal pieces. Add 1 piece of butter to each piece of dough and knead. Brush each roll's surface with olive oil, then, on a floured surface, flatten out each roll. Place 1 tablespoon of olive puree on top of each roll, spread with a knife and roll with your hands.

Cut the dough in half lengthways from just inside one end through to the other end. Twist the strips of dough individually, then twist them together and join ends to make a round roll shape. Place on a non-stick baking tray brushed with oil.

Place the tray in the oven, with the door open, for 20 minutes. The balls will double in size after proofing. Remove tray from oven and turn oven heat up to 180°C (350°F/Gas Mark 4).

Brush egg wash on top of the buns, then sprinkle nigella seeds over the tops. Bake for 25–30 minutes until buns are golden brown.

Sesame Seed Rings
Simit

Every morning in Turkey many people enjoy a simit for breakfast. This traditional dough is sold in rectangular carts on busy walkways and at bus stops during the morning rush hour. The crunchy crust is covered with sesame seeds and the delicious smell attracts anybody passing nearby these small kiosks. Simits are cooked in stone ovens and often eaten with feta cheese and Turkish black tea (see page 151) for a quick but satisfying breakfast.

Makes 4

Ingredients

250 g (8 oz) strong bread flour
½ teaspoon salt
½ teaspoon sugar
½ teaspoon dry yeast
½ cup warm water (approximately)
olive oil
1 tablespoon molasses
½ cup water
sesame seeds

Method

Preheat oven to 220°C (425°F/Gas Mark 7). Sift flour into a large bowl, then add salt and sugar and make a well in the centre.

Mix the yeast with 2 teaspoons of the warm water in the well. Knead all the ingredients with the remaining warm water until the dough is sticky-soft, but not runny. Cover with a tea towel and rest for 30 minutes.

Divide the dough into 4 pieces. Brush the bench with olive oil. You may also need a sprinkle of flour to stop the dough sticking. Tip the dough onto the bench, roll each piece into a long sausage then form into a ring shape and press to seal together.

Stir the molasses into the ½ cup of water in a bowl. Dip the rings in the molasses mixture quickly then dip both sides into sesame seeds.

Place the rings on a greased oven tray and bake for 15 minutes until dark golden.

Mince Meat in Filo Pastry

Kıymalı Gözleme

Gözleme is a classic Turkish pastry prepared for breakfast and lunch or as treats for guests. There are many kinds of fillings for gözleme such as spinach, mash potato, cheese and mince.

We use a very thin special pastry for gözleme called yufka, which is one of the basics of Turkish baking. We roll out the pastry with a thin rolling pin called oklava. You can use your own rolling pin. I reduced the size of the yufka to a 30cm (12 in) diameter for this recipe. Normally it has a diameter of 1 metre (3 feet). Make the yufka first. If you don't have enough time to prepare yufka, you can use 3-ply filo; brush three sheets of filo pastry with oil and layer on top of each other.

Makes 4

Ingredients

Yufka
200 g (7 oz) strong bread flour
20 g (¾ oz) melted butter
¼ teaspoon salt
¼ teaspoon baking powder
100 ml (3½ fl oz) water

Filling
1 onion
5 tablespoons olive oil
500 g (1 lb) minced (ground) beef
1 teaspoon salt

Method

To make yufka: Place all the ingredients into a mixing bowl and mix until you have a soft dough.

Divide into 4 equal pieces; mould each into a ball and leave to rest for 30 minutes. Roll out each ball on a well-floured surface until very thin (about 3 sheets of filo pastry thick) and around 30 cm in diameter.

To make the filling: Chop onion and fry in a saucepan with 3 tablespoons of olive oil. Add mince meat and cook until browned. Add salt.

Divide meat into 4 equal parts and place the mixture in the middle of the yufka. Fold the pastry into envelope shapes.

Heat 2 tablespoons of olive oil in a large frying pan and fry both sides of the gözleme on medium heat until golden brown. Serve hot.

Hot Dog Bundles

Börektas

You will love these soft, delicious bundles. They can be made with feta cheese or olives in the middle instead of frankfurters. You can double the recipe amount and keep half in the freezer. Take them out an hour before you bake them for a picnic or outdoor party.

Makes 20

Ingredients

325 g (11 oz) flour

1¾ teaspoons salt

70 g (2½ oz) cream

1 egg

1 teaspoon sugar

1 teaspoon dry yeast

150 g (5 oz) butter (room temperature)

3 small frankfurters

1 egg, lightly beaten for egg wash

100 g (3½ oz) sesame seeds

Method

Preheat oven to 200°C (400°F/Gas Mark 6).

Sift flour with salt in a mixing bowl. Make a well in the centre and pour in cream, egg and sugar. Dissolve yeast in 1 teaspoon warm water and add to the cream and egg mixture. Add butter in small pieces and knead all the ingredients until you have a soft, smooth dough. Rest dough on a floured surface for 20 minutes.

Cut frankfurter into 5-mm (¼-in) thick pieces. Scoop rounded tablespoons of the dough out and form into a ball using your hands. Push a piece of frankfurter into the middle of each piece of dough and place the hot dog bundles on baking paper and brush with egg wash.

Roll the bundles in the sesame seeds then bake for 20 minutes until golden brown.

Serve warm.

Spinach and Feta Filo Rolls

Kol Böreği

This rich, filled pastry is eaten at every bayram, or festival, in Turkey. Bakers compete to make the thinnest dough and bake the crunchiest pie. It is baked in big, round trays to serve as many people as possible. This filling is the most popular one, but it is also made with minced meat or onion and mashed potato with spices.

Serves 4–6

Ingredients

Dough
250 g (8 oz) plain (all-purpose) flour
½ teaspoon salt
¾ cup milk
extra flour

Filling
500 g (1 lb) fresh spinach
250 g (8 oz) ricotta
½ teaspoon salt
½ teaspoon black pepper
3 eggs
½ cup olive oil

Method

Preheat oven to 200°C (400°F/Gas Mark 6).

To make the pastry: Sift the flour, mix in salt and make a well in the centre. Add milk and knead until you have a slightly firm dough.

Allow to rest for 30 minutes covered with a tea towel.

Combine spinach and ricotta with salt and pepper.

Beat the eggs with the olive oil.

Divide the dough into 4 equal pieces. Roll out each piece into a round on a floured surface, making each as thin as possible. Cut each piece of rolled pastry in half to create two half-circles. Brush with the egg mixture.

Put spinach filling in a line on top of each piece of pastry and roll into long sausage shapes, then coil to make a snail shape and place on a non-stick baking tray brushed with oil. Repeat with the remaining pastry. Brush with remaining egg and olive oil mixture and sprinkle with sesame seeds.

Bake for 30 minutes. Serve hot.

Poppy Seed Treats

Hashasli Kurabiye

Savories are even more welcome than sweet cookies in many parts of Turkey, so we have developed a wide range of these to serve as treats. Poppy seeds have a lovely effect on savory treats. These are also simple to prepare.

Makes 20

Ingredients

350g (12 oz) plain (all-purpose) flour

1¾ teaspoons salt

1 egg

250 g (8 oz) butter

100 g (3½ oz) poppy seed

1 egg, lightly beaten for egg wash

Butterfly cookie cutter

Method

Preheat oven to 180°C (350°F/Gas Mark 4).

Place four and salt in a mixing bowl. Make a well in the centre and add the egg, butter and half of the poppy seeds. Knead until combined. Allow the dough to rest in the fridge for 30 minutes.

Divide the dough into 2 pieces. Roll out onto a floured surface until 1.5 cm (about ½ in) thick. Cut dough with the cutter and spread cookies onto a baking tray lined with baking paper. Brush with egg wash and sprinkle poppy seeds on top. Bake for 25 minutes until golden.

Traditional Turkish Bread

Ramadan Pide

This pide is only sold during the religious month of Ramadan. People queue in front of the bakeries in the late afternoon for the hot, delicious Ramadan pide. Everybody eats this hot bread with dinner for a month. It is especially lovely with butter or thick cream and honey.

Makes 1

Ingredients

500g (1 lb) strong bread flour
1 teaspoon salt
1 teaspoon sugar
375 ml (12 fl oz) warm water
2 teaspoons dry yeast
½ cup water extra
2 tablespoons flour extra

Method

Preheat oven to 70°C (150°F/Gas Mark ¼).

Place flour, salt and sugar in a mixing bowl and make a well centre. Dissolve yeast in the warm water in the well.

Mix until combined and leave to rest for 20 minutes.

Roll the dough into a round shape, tip it onto a floured surface and push it down, making indents with your fingertips. Place on a non-stick baking tray brushed with oil. Place the tray in the oven, with the door open, for 30 minutes. The pide will double in size. Remove tray from oven and turn oven heat up to 200°C (400°F/Gas Mark 6).

Mix flour and water together and brush the mixture onto the pide.

Bake for 15–20 minutes until a light golden colour.

Turkish Mushroom Pizzas

Mantarlı Pide

One of the most well-known Turkish pastries is pide. Pide is made in a variety of shapes, with different ingredients and fillings. Closed ones are like Italian calzone, others are just plain flour ones eaten as bread. Pide with spicy pastrami and egg filling is a mouth-watering version; the feta and parsley filling is a healthier choice. Pide is one of my favourite pastries because it's so diverse. This recipe has a slightly softer dough and a juicy filling. You can also bake one big pide and serve it in slices.

Makes 6

Ingredients

Dough

300 g (10 oz) strong bread flour

200 ml (7 fl oz) warm water

2 teaspoons dry yeast

1 teaspoon sugar

1 tablespoon yogurt

1 teaspoon salt

2 tablespoons olive oil

1 egg, lightly beaten

extra olive oil

Filling

150 g (5 oz) cheddar
  cheese, grated

6 mushrooms, thinly sliced

1 tomato, cubed

dried basil

Method

Preheat oven to 200°C (400°F/Gas Mark 6).

Combine half of the flour and half of the warm water with the yeast in a bowl and combine. Let it rest for 30 minutes covered with a tea towel until bubbles form on the surface. Add the remaining ingredients to this mixture and knead dough on a well-floured surface until smooth and elastic. Cover with tea towel and leave for 30 minutes.

Divide the dough into 8 equal pieces and roll out on an oiled surface. Sprinkle each piece with grated cheddar cheese, sliced mushrooms and tomato. Shape the dough into little 'boats'. Place pide on a greased baking tray and brush with the lightly beaten egg and olive oil.

Bake for 15–20 minutes until golden. Brush with olive oil and sprinkle with basil while still hot.

Sunflower and Sesame Seed Bread

Aycekirdekli Susamli Ekmek

One of my great gourmet recipes for bread lovers. This dense, seed enriched bread will satisfy your appetite at any meal. My choice is to dip it into an Aegean olive oil and a balsamic vinegar. It makes the perfect match for a rocket salad or basil tomato soup.

Makes 2

Ingredients

375 g (12 oz) strong bread flour

650 g (1½ lb) wholewheat flour

1¾ teaspoons salt

50 g (2 oz) dry yeast

650 ml (23 fl oz) warm water

100 g (3½ oz) sultanas

75 g (3 oz) sunflower seeds

75 g (3 oz) sesame seeds

2 teaspoons honey

extra olive oil

extra sunflowers, sultanas, sesame seeds and oats

Method

Sift both types of flour and salt into a large bowl. Make a well in the centre and put the yeast in the well. Pour the warm water slowly into the well. Add the sultanas, seeds and honey and knead until combined. Sift in a little extra flour when you are forming the dough if it's too sticky. Knead for 10 minutes until you have an elastic dough. Make a plus mark in the top of the dough and allow to rest for 30 minutes covered with a tea towel.

Preheat oven to 70°C (150°F). Divide the dough into 2 pieces. Tip onto a floured surface and form both pieces into balls. Place the balls on a tray brushed with oil. Place the tray in the oven, with the door open, for 45 minutes.

Remove tray from oven and turn oven heat up to 200°C (400°F/Gas Mark 6). Brush oil on top of the bread and sprinkle sunflower seeds, sultanas, sesame seeds over the top. Place a small heatproof cup of water into the oven to keep it humid. Bake bread for 10 minutes. Reduce oven temperature to 160°C (325°F/Gas Mark 3) and bake for about 50 minutes until golden brown.

Cinnamon and Sultana Bread Sticks

Uzumlu Tarcinli Ekmek

These crispy stick shaped breads are the ideal match for sweet or savory dishes. I strongly recommend it dipped in chocolate fondue and blended with walnut as well. Also place them in glasses for dips of your choice at party times.

Makes 6

Ingredients

250 g (8 oz) plain
  (all-purpose) flour
25 g (1 oz) cinnamon
250 g (8 oz) wholewheat flour
25 g (1 oz) dry yeast
1 tablespoon honey
375 ml (12 fl oz) warm water
65 g (2½ oz) sultanas
icing sugar

Method

Sift both types of flour and cinnamon into a large bowl. Make a well in the centre and put yeast into the well. Add honey, and pour the warm water into the well to dissolve the yeast. Add sultanas and mix until combined. Knead for about 10 minutes until you have a smooth dough. Allow to rest for 30 minutes covered with a tea towel.

Preheat oven to 70°C (150°F). Divide dough into 6 equal pieces and place on an oily surface, rolling out each piece by hand. Roll each piece into a long, thin sausage shape, then fold into two and twist. Place twisted sticks onto a baking tray brushed with oil. Place the tray in the oven, with the door open, for 45 minutes.

Remove tray from oven and turn oven up to 200°C (400°F/Gas Mark 6). Bake sticks again until golden brown. Sprinkle with icing sugar when cool.

Tahini Bread

Tahinli Pide

Tahini is made from sesame seeds and is extremely nutritious. It is widely used in many of the cookie and bread recipes. My favorite is tahini bread. Tahini bread has its front row position at every Turkish patisserie. The soft ones are delicious fresh and ideal to consume with Turkish black tea as an afternoon treat. You can also use puff pastry if you don't have time to prepare the dough.

Makes 6

Ingredients

Dough

2¹/₃ cups plain (all-purpose) flour

2 teaspoons dry yeast

1 teaspoon salt

3 tablespoons sugar

1 egg

100 g (3½ oz) butter

¾ cup warm water

olive oil

1 egg, lightly beaten for
  egg wash

2 tablespoons sesame seeds,
  for decoration

Filling

250 g (8 oz) tahini

150 g (5 oz) sugar

Method

Preheat oven to 180°C (350°F/Gas Mark 4).

In a small bowl, dissolve the yeast in 2 teaspoons of the warm water. Put all dough ingredients in a bowl and knead until you have a soft dough. Add a little flour as you knead if the dough is too sticky.

Allow to rest for 30 minutes covered with a tea towel.

Cut the dough into 6 equal pieces. Mix together the tahini and sugar. Tip the dough onto an oiled surface and spread out by hand into thin, round shapes. Spread 2 teaspoons of the tahini mixture onto each round shape. Roll the dough into long strips and coil into a snail shape and seal at the end. Place dough onto an oiled baking tray and brush with egg wash.

Sprinkle sesame seeds over the top and bake for 20–25 minutes until golden brown.

Pastry Cigars
Sigara Böreği

Pastry cigars are a familiar sight on Turkish tables. These crunchy, tasty treats make perfect party bites. In Turkey, pastry cigars are made from yufka. If you don't have time to prepare yufka use spring roll pastry or buy yufka, which is available from Turkish grocery shops.

Makes 24

Ingredients

½ bunch of parsley

250 g (8 oz) ricotta cheese

1 teaspoon salt

3 yufka (see recipe page 15) or
  1 packet spring roll pastry

250 ml (8 fl oz) olive oil,
  for frying

Method

Chop parsley and mix with ricotta cheese and salt. Cut pastry into 6 right-angled triangles. Place the ricotta mixture along the long, outer side of each triangle and start to roll. Dip the tip of each cigar into a little water to seal.

Pour olive oil into a deep frying pan and fry the cigars until golden. Serve warm.

Puff Pastry with Chunky Meat

Talaş böreği

This is a traditional Turkish pastry, still offered in some restaurants and Borek shops. It will satisfy the appetite for breakfast or lunch.

Makes 8

Ingredients

3 teaspoons olive oil

1 small onion

500 g (1 lb) beef, diced

150 g (5 oz) (approximately 1 large) grated carrot

150 g (5 oz) peas

1 teaspoon oregano

1 teaspoon salt

1 teaspoon black pepper

2 sheets puff pastry

1 egg, lightly beaten for egg wash

nigella (black cumin) seeds

Method

Preheat oven to 200°C (400°F/Gas Mark 6).

Heat 3 teaspoons oil in a saucepan, add onion and saute. Add meat, carrot, peas, oregano and salt and pepper then cook, stirring over medium heat, about 5–6 minutes. Let cool slightly.

Cut each pastry sheet into 4 equal squares. Put 2 teaspoons of meat filling in the middle of each square and fold pastry into an envelope shape. Use a little water to seal pastry.

Place parcels onto a baking tray brushed with oil. Brush the tops with egg wash and sprinkle nigella seeds over the top.

Bake for 20–25 minutes until golden. Serve hot.

Flat Bread
Bazlama

One of the oldest traditions for Turkish villagers is to prepare their own bread and store it. Bazlama is cooked and kept in a cool place to eat over a few days. Even then, this flat bread is still soft when you warm it up. You can spot the authenticity of this original bread by the thick, round shape.

Makes 4

Ingredients

2 cups strong bread flour
½ teaspoon bicarbonate of soda
1½ cups warm water
1 teaspoon dry yeast
1 tablespoon plain yoghurt
½ teaspoon salt
½ teaspoon sugar

Method

Sift flour and bicarbonate of soda into a mixing bowl and make a well in the centre. Dissolve the yeast into the well with the warm water. Add yoghurt and combine until you have a smooth dough. Rest the dough for 20 minutes.

Divide dough into 4 pieces and roll into balls with your hands. Place on a baking tray, leaving 5 cm (2 in) gaps in between. Allow the dough to rest for 1 hour in a warm place, covered with a tea towel.

Preheat oven to 200°C (400°F/Gas Mark 6) and bake for 20–25 minutes until light golden.

Sarıyer Pastries
Sarıyer Böreği

There are pastry and börek shops selling many kinds of böreks all over Turkey. Each region has its own traditional taste and style. These rich, filled pastries are mainly for breakfast and lunch. Sarıyer Börei is one of my favourite versions. The lovely coastal suburb of Sarıyer has given its name to this delicious pastry.

Makes 6

Ingredients

1 packet of filo pastry

Sauce
2 eggs
50 ml (1½ fl oz) oil
150 ml (5 fl oz) milk

Filling
1 onion, chopped
500 g (1 lb) minced
  beef (ground beef)
5–6 tablespoons olive oil
1 teaspoon salt
1 teaspoon black pepper
½ bunch parsley, chopped
65 g (2½ oz) raisins
50 g (2 oz) pine nuts

Method

Preheat oven to 180°C (350°F/Gas Mark 4).

In a pan, cook chopped onion with meat and olive oil. Add salt, pepper, chopped parsley, raisins and pine nuts. Cook for 5 minutes.

Whisk all sauce ingredients together in a bowl.

Cut the filo pastry sheets into squares. Brush each square with the sauce.

Spread the filling in a straight line along one side of each square and roll. Place the rolled pastries in a U shape on a non-stick tray brushed with oil. Brush the top of the rolls with the remaining sauce. Bake for 30–40 minutes until golden.

Tahini Layers

Katmer

Katmer is my favourite pastry of all time. It's a thin, layer-by-layer pastry and has a sweet flavour. The great thing about katmer is you can eat it with either with jam or cheese and olives, as well as with the dips of your choice. You will be addicted to this recipe.

Makes 6

Ingredients

300 g (10 oz) flour
1¾ teaspoons salt
225 ml (7½ fl oz) water
300 g (10 oz) tahini
50 ml (1½ fl oz) cooking oil

Method

Sift flour and salt into a mixing bowl. Add water and combine until you have a smooth dough. Allow to rest for 20 minutes.

Cut the dough into 4 pieces. Roll out into rounds on a well-floured surface as thin as you can. Spread 3 tablespoons of tahini onto each piece of dough and roll into strips. Coil dough into snail shapes then roll out again until very thin (about 3 sheets of filo pastry thick).

Pour cooking oil into a frying pan and cook the tahini layers on a medium heat until golden.

Black Cumin Seed Pastries

Corek Otlu Kurabiye

Many kinds of savories with different shapes are produced in Turkish bakeries. It is a tradition to buy a box of savories or cookies from a nearby bakery when visiting friends or relatives. Savories are offered to guests along with traditional Turkish tea (see page 151).

Makes 15

Ingredients

250 g (8 oz) flour

1 egg

1 teaspoon salt

150 g (5 oz) butter

150 g (5 oz) grated parmesan cheese

1 egg yolk, lightly beaten for egg wash

1 tablespoon nigella (black cumin) seeds

Method

Preheat oven to 180°C (350°F/Gas Mark 4).

Place all ingredients in a mixing bowl and combine until you have a smooth dough. Roll out dough until 2.5 cm (1 in) thick, and cut into 1.5-cm (½-in) long pieces. Roll each one into a long sausage shape by hand on a floured surface, fold into two and twist, then form into a ring to bind.

Spread the savories on a greased baking tray and brush with egg yolk. Sprinkle nigella seeds over the top and bake for 25–30 minutes until golden brown.

Fork Pastries

Çatal

Çatal is a familiar pastry at every bakery shop and simit stand. It is a soft snack that melts in your mouth. We use mahleb in the recipe, an aromatic spice made from the seeds of the St Lucie Cherry. You can find this spice in gourmet delis or spice sellers. We call the shape of these savories a fork because the first fork savories were 'Y' shaped. Today they are made curved.

Makes 4

Ingredients

2 cups plain (all-purpose) flour
150 g (5 oz) butter
1 egg yolk
1 tablespoon plain yoghurt
1 teaspoon mahleb
1 teaspoon baking powder
nigella (black cumin) seeds
1 egg, lightly beaten for
  egg wash

Method

Preheat oven to 160°C (325°F/Gas Mark 3).

Place all ingredients except egg wash and nigella seeds into a mixing bowl. Mix using an electric mixer with paddle beaters until you have a smooth dough.

Divide dough into 4 equal pieces and tip onto a lightly floured surface. Roll each piece to form a 'U' shape and press the ends of 2 pieces together. Place on a non-stick baking tray brushed with oil. Brush with egg wash and sprinkle black cumin seeds over the top. Bake for 20–25 minutes until golden brown.

Boiled Pastry
Su Böreği

Boiled pastry has a big reputation in Turkish cuisine and bakery. This mouth-watering, layered pastry needs a great deal of effort to prepare, but it is definitely worth it. It tastes a little like cooked pasta, so you can use lasagna sheets instead if you need a quick meal.

Makes 8

Ingredients

4 eggs
2 tablespoons yogurt
2 tablespoons olive oil
500 g (1 lb) plain
  (all-purpose) flour
150 ml (5 fl oz) water
250 g (8 oz) butter
1 bunch parsley, chopped
250 g (8 oz) ricotta cheese
pinch salt

Method

Preheat oven to 180°C (350°F/Gas Mark 4).

Place eggs, yogurt, oil and flour into a mixing bowl. Add water and mix until you have a firm dough. Leave to rest for 20 minutes.

Divide the dough into 6 equal pieces. Roll out each piece on a floured surface until round and very thin (about 3 sheets of filo pastry thick). Set aside two layers for the bottom and top layers.

Boil some water in a large saucepan and prepare a pan of cold water on the side.

Melt butter in a saucepan. Brush a baking tray with olive oil. Place one of the pastry sheets you set aside on the tray and brush pastry well with butter. Divide the rest of the rolled pastries into 2 pieces. Place the pieces into the boiling water and cook for 2 minutes. Soak in cold water and strain.

Mix the parsley with the ricotta and add a pinch of salt.

To assemble: Place the boiled pastry in layers on the tray, brushing each layer well with butter, and spreading with the prepared ricotta and parsley. Repeat for all the layers.

Cover the top with the layer that was set aside. Brush the top with butter. Bake for 15 minutes until golden on top. Turn the tray upside down into another one so that the uncooked part is on top. Continue baking for a further 15 minutes. Serve hot.

Pastrami Pastries

Paçanga

Paçanga is a pie made in Turkish Restaurants and served with a Turkish raki (a kind of liquor made from grape and aniseed). You will never have enough of this crispy-crust pie.

Makes 24

Ingredients

12 sheets filo pastry or
  spring roll pastry
500 g (1 lb) Turkish pastrami
(pastoorma), chopped
250 g (8 oz) grated
  cheddar cheese
50 ml (1½ fl oz) cooking
  (vegetable) oil

Method

Place 3 sheets of filo pastry (or spring roll pastry) onto a lightly floured surface and cut into 4 equal strips, like ribbons.

Brush each pastry ribbon with oil to soften, so that you can fold it without breaking it.

Put some pastrami and cheddar cheese at the top of the pastry ribbon and fold into left side first and then right side to create a triangle shape and continue rolling until you reach the end. Stick the tip together with a little water.

Heat the cooking oil in a deep frying pan on medium heat. Fry the pastrami pastries until golden brown. Serve hot.

Sesame Sticks

Galeta

Turkey is the home of an infinite number of tasty products made of flour. Galeta are extremely delicious crunchy bread sticks and go best with salads or cheese.

Makes 20

Ingredients

2 cups plain (all-purpose) flour

1 teaspoon salt

1 teaspoon sugar

1 teaspoon dry yeast

1/3 cup warm water

2 tablespoons olive oil

sesame seeds

1 egg, lightly beaten for
  egg wash

Method

Preheat oven to 180°C (350°F/Gas Mark 4).

Place flour, salt and sugar in a mixing bowl and make a well in the centre. Place yeast in the well and dissolve with the warm water. Add olive oil and mix until you have a smooth dough. Allow to rest for 30 minutes, covered with a tea towel.

Roll the dough into a 2.5-cm (1-in) thick sausage shape, then slice into 2.5 cm (1-in) long pieces. Roll each piece into a 1-cm (¼-in) thick stick shape.

Place sticks on a non-stick baking tray. Brush with oil and sprinkle sesame seeds over the top.

Bake for 25–30 minutes until golden brown.

Candle Rings

Kandil Simidi

Kandil days are holy days in the Islamic culture. Some people go to mosques and some people stay at home to pray. It is traditional to call on elderly people to celebrate their Kandil. We believe all the prayers made on that day will come true. People buy Kandil Simidi for each other. Kandil Simidi used to be traditional fare on Kandil days four times a year, but nowadays they can be found in patisseries all year round. Two kinds of Kandil Simidi are made; one with sesame and the other with nigella (black cumin) seeds. Mahleb is an aromatic spice and you can find it at spice sellers or gourmet deli shops.

Makes 25

Ingredients

75 g (3 oz) butter

2 eggs

1 teaspoon salt

1 teaspoon sugar

2 cups plain (all-purpose) flour

25 g (1 oz) dry yeast

1 teaspoon mahleb

25 g (1 oz) tahini

200 g (7 oz) sesame seeds

1 egg, lightly beaten for egg wash

Method

Preheat oven to 170°C (325°F/Gas Mark 3).

Place butter and eggs in a mixing bowl, add salt and sugar and mix until combined.

Add flour, yeast dissolved in 1 tablespoon of warm water, mahleb and tahini. Mix well until you have a smooth dough.

Roll the dough into a long sausage shape 2.5 cm (1 in) thick and cut into 2-cm (¾-in) long pieces. Curl each piece to make a ring shape and seal with water to stick.

Brush egg wash on each of the rings and dip into sesame seeds. Place on a non-stick baking tray brushed with oil and bake for 30–35 minutes.

Aniseed Hearts

Anasonlu kurabiye

Another tasty savory recipe that is ideal for parties or picnics. Aniseed hearts are easy to prepare and delicious when served with dips such as guacamole or hummus.

Makes 20

Ingredients

250 g (8 oz) flour
25 g (1 oz) butter
1 teaspoon salt
25 g (1 oz) aniseed
80 ml (2½ fl oz) water

Heart-shaped cookie cutter

Method

Preheat oven to 180°C (350°F/Gas Mark 4).

Place all dry ingredients in a mixing bowl. Add the water and combine until you have a smooth dough. Allow to rest for 30 minutes.

Roll out the dough as thinly as you can. Cut into shapes with the cookie cutter and place on a non-stick baking tray. Bake for 20–25 minutes.

Cookies
& Pastries

Turkish Macaroons

Acibadem Kurabiye

My passion for desserts started with this simple cookie. It might be simple yet irresistible. Two sticky cookies are sandwiched together without any filling, unlike the French version. They can be prepared in smaller or bigger sizes. You will become addicted to these cookies!

Makes 20

Ingredients

150 g (5 oz) almond meal
150 g (5 oz) sugar
2 egg whites
10–12 drops lemon juice

Method

Preheat oven to 130°C (250°F/Gas Mark ½).

Place all ingredients except lemon juice in a saucepan. Using a wooden spoon mix over heat until the sugar is dissolved. Put aside and let cool. Stir in lemon juice.

Spoon the mixture into a piping bag and pipe 3.5 cm (1½ in) rounds onto a non-stick baking tray lined with baking paper.

Bake for 25–30 minutes. Let macaroons cool then sandwich together in twos.

Lemon Meringue Cookies

Limonlu Mereng

The integration of the sticky structure and sweet and sour flavour of this cookie is what makes it unique. These cookies will stay fresh in a closed container for up to a week—if you can hold yourself back.

Makes 20

Ingredients

Pastry

1 egg
65 g (2½ oz) sugar
300 g (10 oz) butter
375 g (12 oz) plain
  (all-purpose) flour
2 teaspoons baking powder

Meringue

4 egg whites
300 g (10 oz) sugar
zest of 2 lemons

Method

To make the pastry: Mix egg and sugar in a bowl with an electric mixer. Add butter and make a creamy mixture. Add the flour and baking powder and knead until you have a smooth dough. If it feels sticky add a little flour. Rest the dough in the fridge for 30 minutes.

To make the meringue: Whip the egg whites for about three minutes, until thick and foamy. Add sugar and whip 2 minutes more. Add lemon zest.

Preheat oven to 160°C (325°F/Gas Mark 3). Roll out the pastry on a well-floured surface in a rectangular shape to about 2 mm thick. Spread meringue over the top in a thin layer using a spatula. Roll the dough to 2-cm (¾-in) thick. Cut into 2cm (¾ in) lengths and place on a non-stick baking tray, leaving 2 cm (¾ in) gaps between them. Bake in oven for 20–25 minutes.

Sesame Seed Cookies

Susamli Kurabiye

I have lots of memories that involve these lovely cookies. I used to pass my fingers through the hole and eat them one by one, it was great fun! Now I cook them for my daughter and I like to see the cookies around her fingers.

Makes 20

Ingredients

1 egg white

125 g (4 oz) icing sugar

175 g (2½ oz) unsalted butter

250 g (8 oz) plain
(all-purpose) flour

¼ teaspoon baking powder

65 g (2½ oz) sesame seeds

1 egg, lightly beaten for
egg wash

5 cm (2 in) round cookie cutter
3 cm (1 in) round cookie cutter

Method

Preheat oven to 180°C (350°F/Gas Mark 4).

Using an electric mixer, whisk the egg white and icing sugar together until creamy. Add the butter and mix for 3 minutes.

Sift the flour and baking powder over the egg and butter mixture. Knead into a dough and turn out onto a floured surface. Using a rolling pin, roll out the dough to a 3mm thickness. Cut the cookies using the larger cutter and make another hole in the middle using the smaller round cutter.

Brush cookies with egg wash and dip into the sesame seeds. Place the cookies a tray lined with baking paper. Bake for 20–25 minutes until lightly golden.

Mushroom Cookies
Mantar Kurabiye

I enjoy preparing these lovely mushroom-shaped cookies and guests love them because of their shape. I use a beer bottle to give them the mushroom shape! Enjoy these mouth-watering cookies with an Earl Grey tea in your afternoons.

Makes 20

Ingredients

1 egg

½ cup + 1 tablespoon sugar

200 g (7 oz) unsalted butter

½ cup plain (all-purpose) flour

3 cups cornflour (cornstarch)

1 teaspoon baking powder

1 tablespoon cocoa powder

Beer bottle, for shaping

Method

Preheat oven to 160°C (325°F/Gas Mark 3).

Using an electric mixer, beat egg, all the sugar and butter until creamy. Sift flour, cornflour (cornstarch) and baking powder over the mixture. Stir lightly with a spoon until combined.

Scoop out rounded tablespoons of the dough and place on a tray lined with baking paper.

Press the beer bottle into the cocoa powder and press down well onto each cookie until you get the shape of a mushroom.

Bake for 20 minutes.

Remove from the oven and allow to cool before eating.

Flour Cookies

Un Kurabiyesi

Flour cookies are my number one cookies. These cookies are certainly the most creative sweet treats of Turkish tradition. I just can't stop myself finishing up the tray. They are so soft that they melt in your mouth.

Makes 15

Ingredients

125 g (4 oz) unsalted butter

4 tablespoons oil

165 g (5¾ oz) plain (all-purpose) flour

150 g (5 oz) cornflour (cornstarch)

100 g (3½ oz) icing sugar

1 teaspoon baking powder

whole almonds, for decoration

extra icing sugar, for dusting

Method

Preheat oven to 150°C (300°F/Gas Mark 2).

Using an electric mixer with paddle beaters, combine all ingredients in a bowl. Let the dough rest for 20 minutes in fridge.

Grab small handfuls of the mixture and roll them in your palm. Place on a non-stick baking tray and push down lightly on the top of the cookies with your finger. Place an almond into each hole.

Bake for 30 minutes. Remove from the oven and let cool. Sprinkle with icing sugar.

Clove, Cinnamon and Ginger Cookies

Uc baharatli Kurabiye

I like the character that cloves introduce to sweets and desserts. These spicy cookies feature a blend of strong spices, including cloves which will make your mouth water as soon as you smell them.

Ingredients

2 teaspoons ground ginger

2 teaspoons cinnamon

2 teaspoons ground cloves

2 tablespoons molasses

250 g (8 oz) flour

65 g (2½ oz) icing sugar

65 g (2½ oz) butter

Cookie cutter

Method

Preheat oven to 170°C (325°F/Gas Mark 3).

Place all spices and molasses in a saucepan and bring to the boil. Remove from stove and let cool.

Use an electric mixer with paddle beaters to mix flour, icing sugar and butter. Add spice liquid and mix until combined. Wrap dough in plastic wrap and place in refrigerator for 30 minutes.

On a lightly floured surface, roll out dough very thinly, about 2 mm (1 in) thick. Cut out shapes with the cookie cutter and place on a non-stick baking tray.

Bake for 20–25 minutes.

Orange Chocolate Cookies

Portakalli Kurabiye

These are my winter cookies; whenever the weather is cold I bake these and make a coffee. They are soft and delicious dark cookies that make a good match with any soft drink, too. They look runny when you take them out after 10 minutes baking time, but they will be all ready once they cool down. Store them in an airtight jar to retain the soft structure.

Makes 25

Ingredients

65 g (2½ oz) butter

½ cup sugar

1 egg

1 cup plain (all-purpose) flour

25 g (1 oz) cocoa powder

2 drops orange essence

Method

Preheat oven to 150°C (300°F/Gas Mark 2).

Using an electric mixer and paddle beaters, cream the butter and sugar. Add egg and beat until mixture is creamy.

Add flour, cocoa powder and orange essence. Stir using a spatula to scrape sides of bowl and mix to combine.

Use a pastry bag fitted with a 1.5 cm (½ in) plain piping nozzle to pipe 2.5 cm (1 in) cookies onto a non-stick baking tray.

Bake for 10 minutes.

Pistachio Cookies

Fistikli Kurabiye

Nature has unbelievable potential. When it comes to the kitchen no one deals with and appreciates this potential like a chef. Pistachio has its own particular taste, colour and flavour and are a crunchy surprise in these cookies. My absolute favourite to serve with an aromatic espresso!

Makes 30

Ingredients

2 eggs

200 g (7 oz) sugar

120 g (3¾ oz) butter

250 g (8 oz) flour

25 g (1 oz) cocoa powder

1 teaspoon bicarbonate soda

50 g (2 oz) pistachio nuts

Method

Preheat oven to 170°C (325°F/Gas Mark 3).

Using an electric mixer and paddle beaters, mix eggs and sugar in a mixing bowl. Add butter and mix until creamy.

Place flour, cocoa powder, bicarbonate of soda and pistachio into the mixing bowl and mix until combined.

Divide the dough into 3 equal pieces. Roll each piece out until 4 cm (1½ in) thick. Mould with your fingers to form a rectangle bread-loaf shape. Place the bread-shaped dough pieces on the back side of a tray and leave them in the freezer for 30 minutes.

Cut into 0.5 cm (¼ in) thin slices. Place cookies on a non-stick baking tray lined with baking paper, allowing a 2.5 cm (1 in) gap between each.

Bake for 20 minutes.

Decorated Heart Cookies

Dekorlu Kalp Kurabiye

These cookies are for special occasions and are a favourite with children! The recipe has the ideal balance of ingredients that will allow you to enjoy your cookies for a week if stored in an airtight jar. You may decorate them in your choice of colours to match the occasion.

Makes 20

Ingredients

Pastry

1 egg white
100 g (3½ oz) icing sugar
130 g (4¼ oz) butter
250 g (8 oz) plain (all-purpose) flour

Icing (Frosting)

1 egg white
300 g (10 oz) icing sugar
pink and red food coloring

Heart-shaped cookie cutter

Method

Preheat oven to 170°C (325°F/Gas Mark 3).

To make the pastry: Using an electric mixer with paddle beaters, to mix egg white and icing sugar until creamy. Add butter and combine at low speed. Add flour and mix until you have a smooth dough. Wrap the dough in plastic wrap and place in the fridge for 30 minutes.

On a lightly floured surface, roll out the dough until 3 mm thick. Using the cutter, cut into cookies and place them on a non-stick baking tray. Bake for 20–25 minutes.

To make the icing: Whisk egg white. Add icing sugar and mix; it needs to be runny. Pour equal amounts of the icing into two bowls. Add pink coloring to one and red coloring to another. You can also make white icing for a third colour.

Using sheets of baking paper, prepare three cones to pipe the icing onto the biscuits. Pipe the icing along the edges and then fill the inside of the cookies according to design and colour of the cookies.

Leave them to set for an hour.

Fried Sugar Pastries

Şekerli Katmer

The origin of this recipe goes back to my childhood. My grandmother used to prepare these pastries when we went to Izmir for school-time holidays. The original version is bigger, but I prefer them in smaller sizes as they are easier to serve. You can serve them with whipped cream and strawberries, or with ice-cream sandwiched between two layers. I always loved the fried dough and sweet combination.

Makes 20

Ingredients

1 cup strong bread flour
½ tablespoon sugar
¼ teaspoon baking powder
¼ teaspoon salt
90 ml (3 fl oz) water
60 ml (2 fl oz) vegetable oil for frying
100 g (3½ oz) icing sugar
10 cm (4 in) round cookie cutter

Method

Place flour, sugar, baking powder and salt into a mixing bowl. Add water and combine until you have a firm dough.

Allow to rest for 30 minutes, covered with a tea towel.

Divide the dough into 2 pieces; roll out each one on a well-floured surface as thinly as you can. The thinner the dough, the crunchier the layers will be. Cut into rounds with the cookie cutter.

Heat cooking oil in a frying pan and fry the pastries at a low heat until they are light golden.

Sprinkle icing sugar over the top when they are hot.

Moon Pies

Ay Çöreği

This rich and wholesome pie is a very old tradition in Turkish patisseries. It is said that this recipe was invented to make use of leftover cake crumbs in the shop by the baker! Today it is a classic. I am sure you will enjoy both making and eating this lovely sweet pie. Earl Grey tea, as usual, is the perfect match for this all-day treat.

Makes 8

Ingredients

Dough

2 eggs

½ cup sugar

2 cups plain (all-purpose) flour

75 g (3 oz) butter

1 teaspoon dry yeast

1 egg yolk, lightly beaten for
  egg wash

Filling

2 cups chocolate cake crumbs

1 teaspoon cinnamon

½ cup walnuts

½ cup sultanas

zest of 1 orange

½ cup water

Method

Preheat oven to 180°C (350°F/Gas Mark 4).

To make the dough: Place eggs, sugar, flour and butter in a mixing bowl. Place the yeast in a small bowl or cup and stir in 2 tablespoons of warm water to dissolve. Add to the bowl with the flour. Mix until you have a soft dough. Leave it to rest for 20 minutes.

To make the filling: Using an electric mixer with paddle beaters, mix all the filling ingredients, adding the water slowly to combine.

Divide the dough into 8 equal pieces and roll out each into rounds about 2.5 cm (1 in) thick. Place 2 tablespoons of filling onto each round and form into horseshoe shapes and press tips to seal. Place pies onto a non-stick baking tray brushed with oil. Wash with egg yolk and bake pies for 25 minutes until golden brown.

Linseed and Sunflower Cookies

Keten Tohumlu, Ay Cekirdekli Kurabiye

Less sugar and more grain! These are perfectly healthy cookies. I have also prepared these cookies with diabetic sugar and they still tasted great. Store them in a cookie jar for up to ten days and they'll stay fresh and delicious. I strongly recommend that you prepare all of my cookies to experience the perfect chemistry of the ingredients. You will immediately notice the difference between an industrial and a healthy homemade recipe!

Makes 20

Ingredients

1 egg

100 g (3½ oz) icing sugar

200 g (7 oz) butter

250 g (8 oz) flour

65 g (2½ oz) linseed, sunflower seeds, oats mix

1 egg white, lightly beaten for egg wash

½ cup sunflower seeds for decoration

Daisy-shaped cookie cutter

Method

Preheat oven to 180°C (350°F/Gas Mark 4).

Using an electric mixer with paddle beaters, mix egg and icing sugar. Add butter and mix until creamy.

Add flour, linseed and sunflower seeds and combine until you have a smooth dough. Roll out the dough on a floured surface until it is 3 mm thick.

Cut into shapes with a cookie cutter and place on a baking tray lined with baking paper, leaving 2.5 cm (1 in) gaps in between. Brush with egg wash and sprinkle some sunflower seeds over the top.

Bake for 20–25 minutes until light golden brown.

Raspberry Rolls

Frambuazli Rulolar

These rolls carry the fresh flavour of mountain raspberries and are an interesting treat for your guests.

Makes 30

Ingredients

150 g (5 oz) butter
50 g (2 oz) icing sugar
1 egg
200 g (7 oz) plain
  (all-purpose) flour
½ teaspoon baking powder
100 g (3½ oz) raspberry jam
zest of 1 lemon

Method

Preheat oven to 170°C (325°F/Gas Mark 3).

Using an electric mixer and paddle beaters, combine butter, icing sugar, and lemon zest. Add egg and mix at low speed until creamy. Add flour and baking powder mix until combined.

Allow the dough to rest in fridge for 30 minutes.

Roll out the dough until very thin (about 3 sheets of filo pastry thick). Spread the jam over the dough using a spatula. Roll the dough up into a frankfurter shape and let it rest for 20 minutes in the fridge.

Slice the dough into 3 mm discs and place on a non-stick baking tray.

Bake for 8–10 minutes until light golden.

Turkish Apple Rolls
Elmali Kurabiye

Who doesn't like a classic apple pie? Turkish apple rolls are a creative alternatives for the combined taste of apple and baked dough. Their cookie-shaped size makes them easy to serve and store for longer periods. And no one can tell how many you've eaten!

Makes 12

Ingredients

Dough

2 cups plain (all-purpose) flour

½ cup icing sugar

200 g (7 oz) butter, room temperature

2 tablespoons plain yogurt

Filling

4 apples

2 tablespoons butter

1 teaspoon cinnamon

¼ cup sultanas

extra icing sugar to dust

Method

Preheat oven to 170°C (325°F/Gas Mark 3).

To make dough: Place all ingredients in a mixing bowl and stir until combined. Leave for 20 minutes in the fridge.

To make the filling: Peel then dice the apples. Melt butter in a saucepan. Add apple, cinnamon and sultanas. Cook for 5–6 minutes. Roll out the dough until very thin (about 3 sheets of filo pastry thick), and cut into 12 triangles. Put a tablespoonful of filling on the edge of each triangle and roll up.

Place rolls on a non-stick baking tray. Bake for 25–30 minutes. Leave to cool then sprinkle with icing sugar.

Hazelnut Stars

Findikli Yildiz Kurabiye

Hazelnut is such a unique flavor and I can't imagine what chefs would be using without the strong, bitter taste of a mature almond; it has its own spirit and enriches any combination. My hazelnut stars will give you a simple yet rich taste through the integration of butter and almond along with the classic cinnamon.

Makes 25

Ingredients

1 egg white

150 g (5 oz) butter

200 g (7 oz) plain (all-purpose) flour

100 g (3½ oz) hazelnut meal

2 teaspoons cinnamon

100 g (3½ oz) icing sugar

150 g (5 oz) milk chocolate, for icing (frosting)

Star-shaped cookie cutter

Method

Preheat oven to 180°C (350°F/Gas Mark 4).

Using an electric mixer with paddle beaters, mix the egg white, icing sugar and butter in a mixing bowl until creamy. Place flour, hazelnut meal and cinnamon into the bowl and mix at low speed until combined. Transfer the dough to the fridge until firm, about 20 minutes.

Roll out the dough to a 3mm thickness on a lightly floured surface. Cut into star shapes using a cookie cutter.

Place on a non-stick baking tray and bake for 20–25 minutes. Leave to cool.

Melt chocolate in a bain-marie or microwave. Using a knife, spread the chocolate on top of the cookies and leave to set.

Sweet Almond Horseshoe Pies

Bademli Pay

Another perfect indulgence created with almond. The combination of delicious almond paste and soft pastry literally melts in the mouth.

Makes 8

Ingredients

Almond paste
1 egg white
120 g (3¾ oz) icing sugar
150 g (5 oz) almond meal
40 g (1½ oz) butter

Dough
2 cups (all-purpose) flour
½ cup icing sugar
200 g (7 oz) butter
2 tablespoons yoghurt
extra sugar, for dusting

Method

Preheat oven to 170°C (325°F/Gas Mark 3).

To make the almond paste: Place all ingredients in a mixing bowl and stir until combined. Set aside.

To make the dough: Place all ingredients in a mixing bowl and knead until you have a firm dough.

Divide the dough into 8 equal pieces. Roll out each piece until very thin (about 3 sheets of filo pastry thick). Divide almond paste into 8 equal pieces. Roll them to a finger thickness, place on the edge of each piece of dough and roll up. Form each piece into a horseshoe shape and sprinkle with sugar.

Place pies on a baking tray lined with baking paper. Bake for 25–30 minutes until golden.

Tarts
& Cakes

Almond Peach Tart

Seftali ve bademli Tart

Fresh summer fruit is a favourite choice in desserts. I have created this fine tasting tart by blending almond paste and peaches and balancing the rich tastes of almond, peach and the crispy dough. Consider adding a large scoop of vanilla ice-cream for the ultimate dessert.

Serves 6

Ingredients

Pastry
1 egg
200 g (7 oz) butter
100 g (3½ oz) icing sugar
300 g (10 oz) plain
  (all-purpose) flour

Almond Cream
2 eggs
100 g (3½ oz) sugar
75 g (3 oz) butter
100 g (3½ oz) almond meal

2 fresh peaches

Method

Preheat oven to 180°C (350°F/Gas Mark 4).

Line a 28 cm (11 in) tart pan with a removable base with baking paper.

To make shortbread pastry: Using an electric mixer with paddle beaters, combine the egg and butter, then add the icing sugar and mix until creamy. Add flour and mix until combined. Transfer to the fridge for 20 minutes.

To make almond cream: Using an electric mixer with paddle beaters, mix eggs and sugar in a mixing bowl. Add butter and mix until creamy. Add almond meal and mix until combined. Cover with cling wrap and transfer to the fridge for about 15 minutes.

Roll out the pastry on a lightly floured surface until 3 mm thick. Place into the tart pan. Spoon almond cream into a piping bag with a nozzle and fill the tart shell, leaving a ½ cm space at the top.

Cut peaches in thin slices and place on top of the filling. Bake for 45–50 minutes until golden.

Chocolate Mousse Tart

Cikolatali Tart

A classic of dessert art, in this recipe I have brought together the rich flavour of Grand Marnier and creamy dark chocolate for the ultimate mouth-watering experience. One can easily finish up half of the tart due to its reduced sugar amount. Although a latte or cappuccino seems best suited to this classic tart I recommend the Turkish Earl Grey tea for its neutral taste, to get the maximum flavour from your tart.

Serves 6

Ingredients

Shortbread pastry

1 egg
100 g (3½ oz) icing sugar
200 g (7 oz) butter
300 g (10 oz) flour

Filling

150 g (5 oz) chocolate
100 g (3½ oz) cream
2 eggs

25 g (1 oz) sugar
2 tablespoons Grand Marnier

Method

Preheat oven to 180°C (350°F/Gas Mark 4).

Line a 28 cm (11 in) tart pan with a removable base with baking paper.

Prepare shortbread pastry first (see recipe method page 78). Roll out on a lightly floured surface until 3 mm thick. Press the pastry into a tart pan with a removable base.

To make the filling: Melt chocolate in a bain-marie or microwave. Allow to cool. Using an electric mixer with whisk attachments, whisk cream until fluffy. Transfer it to another mixing bowl. Place eggs in the cleaned mixing bowl and whisk at high speed. Add sugar and whip until creamy.

Combine cream and egg mixture using a wooden spoon. Add chocolate and mix gently. Be careful that it doesn't collapse. Stir in Grand Marnier and pour the filling into the tart shell. Refrigerate for at least 3 hours before serving.

Chocolate Fig Tart

Incirli Tart

I believe you will get everything you want from this creative chocolate tart. In this recipe Turkish dried fig has its own unique flavour that is enriched with a perfectly balanced chocolate filling. This sweet gourmet tart will linger in the memories of your guests.

Serves 8

Ingredients

Shortbread Pastry

1 egg
100 g (3½ oz) icing sugar
200 g (7 oz) butter
300 g (10 oz) flour

Chocolate Filling

100 g (3 oz) dark chocolate
3 eggs
65 g (2½ oz) butter
50 g (2 oz) sugar
25 g (1 oz) cocoa powder
50 g (2 oz) almond meal
12 fresh or dry figs, leave whole

Method

Preheat oven to 180°C (350°F/Gas Mark 4).

Line a 28 cm (11 in) tart pan with a removable base with baking paper.

To make shortbread pastry: Mix icing sugar and butter in a mixing bowl then add egg and sifted flour. Make a soft dough. Rest the dough in the refrigerator for 10 minutes. Roll out on a slightly floured surface until 3 mm thick. Press the pastry into the tart pan.

To make the filling: Melt the chocolate in a bain-marie or microwave oven on low. Allow to cool.

Using an electric mixer with whisk attachments, beat the eggs, then add butter and sugar, mixing until creamy. Pour in melted chocolate at low speed. Add cocoa powder and almond meal and mix until combined.

Pour the filling into the tart shell and place figs on top. Bake for 30 minutes. Refrigerate tart for at least two hours before serving.

Pumpkin Cake

Balkabakli Pasta

Pumpkin is the inspiration for the main filling of this lovely cake. The pureed pumpkin boiled with sugar creates a unique flavour and is a rich component in this cake. Surprise your guests with the rich taste and colorful layers of this creative cake.

Serves 8

Ingredients

750 g (1½ lb) pumpkin
1½ cups sugar
sponge cake (see recipe page 91)
500 ml (18 fl oz) cream
150 g (5 oz) crushed walnuts

Method

Place pumpkin and sugar in a saucepan, add ½ cup water and boil for 20–25 minutes over medium heat.

Prepare the sponge cake and pour into a 24 cm (9½ in) cake tin. Bake for 20 minutes. Cut into 3 layers when cool.

Blend cooked pumpkin to make a puree. Set aside ⅓ of the pumpkin mixture for glazing.

Using an electric mixer, whip the cream until fluffy. Using a spatula, spread cream over the first layer of cake, spread some pumpkin puree over the top then sprinkle with crushed walnuts. Repeat for the second layer of cake then place the last layer on top.

Spread the rest of the cream over the top and sides of the cake in a thin layer. Set in the freezer for about 1 hour.

Remove from the freezer, cover the cake with the pumpkin puree and put back in the freezer for another hour. Move to the refridgerator an hour before serving.

Yogurt Cake
Yogurtlu Pasta

Plain yogurt is consumed more then milk in Turkey. It is served with many dishes and even consumed as a drink, called 'ayran', when blended with water.

Yogurt as an ingredient has many uses for savory recipes, but here I've used this highly nutritious product into an original and tasty cake.

Makes 6

Ingredients

1 egg

100 g (3½ oz) sugar

200 g (7 oz) plain Turkish or Greek yogurt

250 g (8 oz) whipped cream

1 tablespoon gelatin

juice of a half lemon

6 x 5 cm (2 in) round cake moulds

extra whipped cream

extra icing sugar

Lady Fingers

65 g (2½ oz) egg white (approximately 2 eggs)

40 g (1½ oz) sugar

50 g (2 oz) egg yolk

3½ tablespoons plain (all-purpose) flour

25 g (1 oz) cornflour (cornstarch)

Method

Beat egg and sugar using an electric mixer until soft peaks form. Add yogurt and mix until combined.

Dissolve gelatin in 3 teaspoons of water and stir into the mixture. Add the whipped cream and lemon juice.

Sprinkle icing sugar into 6 individual cake moulds; this makes it easy to remove the cakes later. Pour the yoghurt mixture into the moulds and freeze for 3 hours. Take out 30 minutes before serving.

To make lady fingers: Preheat oven to 200°C (400°F/Gas Mark 6). Beat the egg white with an electric mixer until fluffy. Add sugar and egg yolk and beat until thick. Stir in the flour and cornflour with a spatula.

Spoon mixture into a piping bag with an 8 mm (1/3 in) nozzle. Pipe flowers and straight lines with the mixture onto baking paper. Bake for 5–6 minutes until light brown. Leave to cool.

Remove the cakes from the molds, sprinkle with icing sugar. Pipe whipped cream on top of the yoghurt cake and decorate with the lady fingers.

Chocolate Cake
Cikolatali Kek

These cakes are the ultimate chocolate experience. They have a muddy texture and a rich dark chocolate flavour. I love the simplicity of this recipe that brings out the taste of chocolate with the always magical effects of eggs.

Makes 4

Ingredients

200 g (7 oz) dark chocolate
3 eggs

4 silicon moulds

Method

Preheat oven to 150°C (300°F/Gas Mark 2).

Melt the chocolate in a bain-marie or microwave on low heat. Cool slightly but don't let it solidify.

Beat the eggs well with an electric mixer until thick and fluffy. Add chocolate, beating at low speed.

Spread the mixture evenly into the moulds and bake for 17 minutes. The cakes will rise in the centre but will set when they cool down.

Remove from moulds when cool and serve with vanilla ice-cream.

Pyramid Cake
Piramit Pasta

Pyramid cakes are the most eye-catching cakes when you enter a Turkish patisserie. The shape makes it popular with children who like to make their mother prepare it at home—I know I did. Once it is cut into slices, the crunchy biscuits dipped in the intense chocolate are irresistible.

Ingredients

Chocolate Cream

2 tablespoons flour

2 tablespoons cornflour (cornstarch)

2 tablespoons cocoa powder

3 cups milk

¾ cup sugar

25 g (1 oz) butter

1 egg

100 g (3½ oz) bitter chocolate

Cake

500 g (1 lb) plain biscuits

cocoa powder, for decoration

200 g (7 oz) crushed nuts, for decoration

Method

To make chocolate cream: Place all ingredients except the chocolate into a saucepan and stir continuously over low heat until thick. Remove from the stove, add chocolate and stir until combined. Set aside ¼ of chocolate cream to cover the cake.

Break the biscuits into pieces and stir through the remaining ¾ of the warm chocolate cream. Place a large sheet of foil on a tray. Spread the mixture in the middle of the foil in a rectangular shape. Shape it into a pyramid shape using the edges of the foil. Refrigerate for 3 hours.

Using a spatula, cover the cake with the rest of the chocolate cream. Sprinkle cocoa powder over the top and decorate with nuts.

Chestnut Cake
Kestaneli Pasta

The taste of the chestnut is enhanced by the ingredients that dissolve in it. In this recipe the chestnut absorbs the excess sugar. The tasty ganache is lightened by the combination of the chestnut paste and it forms a fabulous gourmet cake.

Ingredients

Sponge Cake

5 eggs
125 g (4 oz) sugar
125 g (4 oz) plain (all-purpose) flour

Ganache

150 g (5 oz) dark chocolate
700 ml (23 fl oz) cream
1 tablespoon rum

Chestnut Paste

500 g (1 lb) dark chocolate
65 g (2½ oz) butter
500 ml (18 fl oz) cream
500g (1 lb) chestnut puree (from gourmet supermarkets)
whole chestnuts, for decoration

Method

Preheat oven to 180°C (350°F/Gas Mark 4).

To make the sponge cake: Using an electric mixer, whip the eggs until firm. Add sugar and mix. Stir in flour gently using a spatula. Grease and line the base of a 20 cm (8 in) round spring-form cake pan with non-stick baking paper. Pour in sponge cake mixture and bake for 20–25 minutes.

To make the ganache: Melt chocolate in a bain-marie or microwave. Allow to cool. In a separate bowl, using an electric mixer, whip the cream until fluffy. Pour chocolate over whipped cream and mix gently with a spatula. Stir in rum. Be careful not to overmix or it will separate.

To make the chestnut paste: Melt chocolate in a bain-marie or microwave on low heat. Add butter and mix with a spatula. Add cream and chestnut paste and mix.

Line a 24 cm (9½ in) dome-shaped cake tin with plastic wrap. Slice sponge cake into 3 equal layers. Place one layer into the cake pan. Spread with a layer of ganache filling and then a layer of chestnut paste. Cover with another layer of sponge cake and spread again with both fillings. Top with a layer of sponge cake.

Refrigerate the cake for 3–4 hours then remove carefully from the pan by tipping it upside down and place on a wire rack. Melt the ganache in a bain-marie or microwave and spread another layer of ganache filling on top of the cake. Refrigerate for another hour.

Pour the ganache over the top of the cake and leave it to set. Transfer cake to a serving plate and decorate with chestnuts.

Plum Cake
Erikli Kek

Plums have an original sweet and sour flavour and, like most other fruit, they taste even better when baked. This recipe is balanced to bring together these qualities for a light and mouth-watering experience.

Ingredients

2 eggs

1⅓ cups sugar

180 g (3 oz) butter

½ cup milk

½ cup warm water

2 cups plain (all-purpose) flour

½ teaspoon bicarbonate of soda

½ teaspoon salt

200 g (7 oz) fresh plums

Method

Preheat oven to 180°C (350°F/Gas Mark 4).

Using an electric mixer, beat eggs in a mixing bowl on medium speed. Add sugar and beat until mixture is thick. Add butter, warm water and milk and the dry ingredients. Mix until combined.

Pour the mixture into a non-stick cake pan. Cut the plums in half. Spread plums over the mixture. Bake for 40–45 minutes. Leave to cool then take cake out of the pan after 10 minutes. Leave to cool down and sprinkle with icing sugar to serve.

Raspberry Millefeuille Cake

Milfoy Pasta

The well known millefeuille cake is here enriched with the classic taste of almond cake and the tang of juicy raspberries.

Serves 8

Ingredients

Vanilla Cream
1 L (2 pints) milk
1 cup plain (all-purpose) flour
25 g (1 oz) cornflour (cornstarch)
2 eggs
seeds from 1 vanilla pod
1 cup sugar
50 g (2 oz) butter
300 g (10½ oz) whipped cream

Almond Cake
5 egg whites
25 g (1 oz) icing sugar
5 egg yolks
100 g (3½ oz) sugar
50 g (2 oz) plain (all-purpose) flour
65 g (2½ oz) almond meal
2 puff pastry sheets
250 g (8 oz) raspberries
icing sugar, for decoration.

Method

To make the vanilla cream: Place all ingredients except butter and cream in a large saucepan. Whisk continuously over medium heat on the stovetop until the mixture boils and thickens. Remove from heat when you see bubbles. Add the butter and whisk. Leave to cool. Using an electric mixer with paddle beaters, beat cream at high speed until fluffy. Add vanilla cream and whip at low speed for 3 minutes.

Preheat oven to 200°C (400°F/Gas Mark 6). Bake two sheets of puff pastry for 15–20 minutes until golden. Leave to cool.

To make the almond cake: Preheat oven to 220°C (425°F/Gas Mark 7). Using an electric mixer, beat egg whites until fluffy. Add icing sugar and beat until thick. Pour the mixture into a large bowl.

In a separate bowl beat egg yolks and sugar until creamy. Stir egg yolk mixture into egg whites in the large bowl using a spatula. Gently stir in flour and almond meal. Spread the mixture into a 28 cm x 43 cm (11 in x 17 in) standard baking tray lined with baking paper and bake for 7 minutes. Leave cake to cool. To separate easily from the baking paper, turn the cake over and brush the other side of the paper with water. Cut the cake in half lengthways.

To assemble: Cut the puff pastry sheets to the same size as the cake. Place the cake at the bottom. Pour vanilla cream into a piping bag and pipe onto the cake. Spread raspberries over the top of the cream. Repeat the layering of cake, cream and raspberries then top with pastry. Sprinkle with icing sugar and decorate with raspberries. Serve immediately.

Banana Coconut Cake

Muzlu Hindistan Cevizli Pasta

This cake is one of my sweetest childhood memories and even now it's still my favourite. I like the combination of the two tropical flavours; banana and coconut. It makes a wonderful birthday cake. Cake cream is commonly used in Turkish patisseries instead of whipped cream. We always use sponge cake with layers and put various fruits, nuts and pistachios in between. It is a lovely to experience a rich, juicy Turkish cake with a glass of Turkish tea.

Serves 6

Ingredients

vanilla cream (see page 95)
sponge cake (see page 91)
3 bananas
100g shredded coconut

Method

Make the vanilla cream and sponge cake as per the recipes.

Slice sponge cake into 3 layers. Spread vanilla cream and banana slices onto first layer. Place the second layer of sponge cake on top and repeat with the cream and banana.

Put the third layer on top and spread the cream to a thin layer using a spatula. Sprinkle coconut over the sides and top.

Refrigerate for 3 hours before serving.

Desserts

Milky Chocolate Pudding

Supangle

This may be the favourite pudding of Turkish children. As a tradition this chocolate pudding comes with a surprise cake slice within.

Makes 4

Ingredients

Pudding

2 cups milk

2 teaspoons cornflour
  (cornstarch)

¾ cup sugar

100 g (3½ oz) chocolate

2 drops vanilla essence

1 teaspoon butter

3 teaspoons cocoa powder

raspberries, for decoration

Raspberry Sauce

150 g (5 oz) raspberries

⅓ cup water

1 teaspoon cornflour
  (cornstarch)

Method

To make raspberry sauce: Place all ingredients in a saucepan and boil until thickened. Pour about 1 cm (½ in) of raspberry sauce into the serving cups or ramekins. Refrigerate for 20 minutes until set.

To make milk pudding: Place all ingredients except butter and cocoa in a pan and boil until thickened. Remove from heat and stir in butter and cocoa. Pour the pudding over the top of the raspberry sauce. Refrigerate at least 2 hours before serving.

Mango Dairy Desert
Muhallebi

In Turkey we have many different kinds of dairy desserts that are popular because of their lightness. Muhallebi is a favourite and special muhallebi shops sell these dairy products on every corner. Most Turkish babies grow up on muhallebi. It often came to my rescue when my baby didn't want to eat her food. I prepare this creamy dessert with a colourful, tropical touch.

Serves 6

Ingredients

Muhallebi

200 ml (7 fl oz) water

1 L (2 pints) milk

50 g (2 oz) cornflour
(cornstarch)

25 g (1 oz) flour

150 g (5 oz) sugar

extra mango cubes

extra desiccated coconut

Mango Sauce

250 g (8 oz) mango puree

200 ml (7 fl oz) water

2 teaspoons cornflour
(cornstarch)

75 g (3 oz) sugar

Method

Prepare 6 individual serving cups or moulds by first dipping the edges into water and then coconut.

To make muhallebi: Combine all the ingredients for muhallebi in a saucepan and boil the mixture, stirring, until you see bubbles. Pour the hot muhallebi into the serving cups and leave to cool. Put in the refrigerator for 30 minutes.

To make mango sauce: Put all the ingredients into a saucepan. Boil the mixture until you see bubbles and the mixture thickens slightly.

Pour a 2 cm (¾ in) layer of sauce slowly over the cold muhallebi. Cool in the fridge for 2–3 hours and decorate with mango cubes before serving.

Kadayıf

Kadayıf is shredded dough and looks a bit like vermicelli noodles—very thin and wiry. It is available from Turkish or Greek grocery stores and suppliers, It is a very decorative ingredient for desserts. This is the classic and most popular kadayıf recipe in Turkey. You can also bake the dessert instead of frying for a lighter alternative.

Makes 6

Ingredients

500 g (1 lb) kadayıf
200 g (7 oz) crushed
  pistachio nuts

Syrup
2 cups sugar
2 cups water
juice of half a lemon

Method

To make the syrup: Place water and sugar into a saucepan and boil until you have a rich, thick syrup. Add the lemon juice. Set aside ¼ of the syrup.

Place the kadayıf into a bowl, pour the hot syrup over it and let cool.

Pull off pieces of the kadayıf as big as your palm. Put crushed pistachios in the middle of them and shape into a rectangular roll.

Place the rolls in a deep tray. Pour the rest of the syrup onto the kadayıf. Wait until they soak up the syrup.

Serve with double cream and crushed pistachios.

If you prefer to back the kadayif, preheat oven to 180°C (350°F/Gas Mark 4) and bake for 25 mintues or until it is golden in colour.

Pumpkin Dessert

Kabak Tatlısı

Are you ready for an unusual dessert? You'll love this once you taste it. It is a classic for New Year celebrations in my country. You can cook this practical dessert on a stove top in a pan instead of using the oven; you won't get a brown crust like the one from the oven but it will taste just as good.

Serves 6

Ingredients

500 g (1 lb) Kent (Jap) pumpkin
1¼ cups sugar
150 g (5 oz) crushed walnuts
150 g (5 oz) whipped cream or
    vanilla ice-cream

Method

Preheat oven to 180°C (350°F/Gas Mark 4).

Peel the pumpkin and cut into spoonful-sized pieces.

Place pumpkins in an oven dish and sprinkle with the sugar. Bake pumpkins until they are soft and brown at the top of the oven for 40–45 minutes.

Leave pumpkin to cool then refrigerate for 2 hours. Serve with whipped cream or vanilla ice-cream with crushed walnuts sprinkled on top.

Ricotta Cheese Dessert

Höşmerim

Höşmerim has many different versions in the Thrace region. It's a very tasty and light cheese dessert that is quick and easy to make. You can serve it with fruit sauces and ice-cream or even with whipped cream.

Serves 4

Ingredients

2 cups milk
125 g (4 oz) sugar
150 g (5 oz) ricotta cheese
65 g (2½ oz) semolina
a few threads of saffron

Method

Preheat oven to 180°C (350°F/Gas Mark 4).

Place milk, sugar and ricotta cheese in a saucepan and bring to the boil. Add semolina and continue heating until the mixture is warm and thicker and bubbles are starting to form.

Add a little bit saffron for a yellow hue. Transfer to 20 cm (8 in) diameter oven dish and bake for 20 minutes until golden brown on the top. Serve cool.

Baked Semolina

Revani

This spongy and wet cake is the favorite dessert during festival days known as bayram. It is extremely yummy with double cream or ice-cream.

Serves 8

Ingredients

2 eggs
2 cups milk
1½ cups semolina
1 cup sugar
1 cup plain (all-purpose) flour
1 teaspoon bicarbonate of soda

pistachios, for decoration

Syrup
3 cups sugar
4 cups water
1 teaspoon lemon juice

Method

Preheat oven to 180°C (350°F/Gas Mark 4).

To make syrup: Place sugar, water and lemon juice in a saucepan and boil for 25 minutes until it thickens. Remove from stove and leave to cool.

Using an electric mixer with paddle beaters, mix eggs, milk and sugar in a bowl at low speed until sugar is dissolved. Add the other ingredients and mix until combined.

Pour the mixture into a deep, non-stick, rectangular baking tray. Bake for 20 minutes. Remove from oven and cut into diagonal slices. Bake for another 10–15 minutes until golden brown.

Pour cool syrup over the hot revani and leave for 30 minutes until the syrup is soaked up. Decorate with pistachio nuts and serve cool.

Baklava

This popular dessert may have its roots across the Middle East; on the other hand it was perfected in the Ottoman Era by the Turks. This syrupy version is a taste sensation, combining crusty top and bottom layers with a soft and nutty middle to die for.

Serves 8

Ingredients

1 package filo pastry
1½ cups milk
25 g (1 oz) semolina
400 g (13 oz) butter
250 g (8 oz) ground pistachios

Syrup
3 cups sugar
2 cups water

Method

Preheat oven to 200°C (400°F/Gas Mark 6).

Boil milk and semolina in a saucepan for 10 minutes. Set aside to cool. Melt butter in another saucepan. Cut the pastry to fit the size of a deep baking tray measuring 25 cm x 35 cm (10 in x 14 in).

Place half of the pastry sheets into the tray, brushing each sheet with butter. Spread cooled semolina mixture onto the pastry, then sprinkle ground pistachios over the top. Cover with other half of the pastry, brushing each sheet with butter.

Use any leftover cut pastry on the top. Cut baklava in diagonal shapes.

Pour butter on top. Bake for 20–30 minutes until golden brown. Cut through the pastry again along the diagonal lines while hot. Leave to cool.

To make syrup: Boil water and sugar in a saucepan for about 30 minutes over medium heat until it gets thick and syrupy. Pour hot syrup over cool baklava with a ladle. Leave to cool and serve.

Ottoman Dessert
Tulumba

An Ottoman classic, you will love this crunchy, golden, fried dough. Pay special attention to the temperature of the oil; it should be warm rather than hot. You may need to remove your pan from the heat if the oil becomes too hot. The syrup needs to be cold when you pour it over the hot tulumba.

Serves/Makes 8

Ingredients

2½ cups water
125 g (4 oz) butter
1 teaspoon sugar
1 teaspoon salt
2 cups plain (all-purpose) flour
4 eggs
2 tablespoons semolina
2 tablespoons rice flour
3 cups vegetable oil

Syrup
3 cups sugar
3 cups water
juice of ½ a lemon

Method

To make the syrup: Place sugar and water into a saucepan and boil over medium heat. Add lemon juice. Keep boiling until the syrup thickens, about 20–25 minutes. Leave to cool.

Place water in a saucepan and add butter, sugar and salt and boil for 5 minutes. Add flour slowly into the mixture using a whisk. Remove from the stove and cool until the mixture is warm.

Add eggs one by one and mix well. Add semolina and rice flour and mix well again.

Place cooking oil in a pan and warm it up on low heat so it is warm, not hot. Pour the dough into a piping bag and pipe 5-cm (2-in) lengths directly into the warm oil. Fry until bright and golden. Place the fried dough into the syrup and let soak for 15 minutes. Serve cool.

Oven-Cooked Rice Pudding

Fırın Sütlaç

Sütlaç is a favourite milky dessert among Turkish people. It is a national tradition to go to dessert shops, especially after dinner. During the long and hot summer nights, Sütlaç, like other traditional milky desserts, is eaten with ice-cream followed by Turkish tea. The burnt caramel on top of this commonly known pudding shows its unique Turkish character.

Makes 4

Ingredients

500 ml (18 fl oz) milk
65 g (2½ oz) sugar
50 g (2 oz) rice
3 tablespoons rice flour
2 tablespoons cornflour
    (cornstarch)
½ teaspoon salt
1 tablespoon butter

Method

Preheat oven to 180°C (350°F/Gas Mark 4).

In a saucepan, boil 400 ml (14 fl oz) of the milk, sugar and rice together until rice is soft. Using a whisk, mix the remaining 100 ml (3 $^1/_3$ fl oz) of milk with the rice flour and cornflour.

Pour this flour mixture slowly into the rice mixture. Add salt and stir continuously until the sütlaç is thickened.

Remove from the stove and stir in the butter. Pour into 4 individual baking cups/moulds and bake until the top of the sütlaç turns brown. Serve cold.

Aşure

This is one of the most interesting of Turkish desserts. It is believed that Noah, at the end of the great flood, ordered a soup to be prepared from what was left in the store of the ark. So aşure came about, with its sweet taste and a wide range of ingredients. According to popular culture, a good aşure should have 40 different ingredients! I prefer to cook it with less ingredients.

This dessert is prepared on a specific date called Aşure Day, which is on the 10th of Muharrem—the first month of the lunar year. It is shared with neighbours, relatives and guests. It may appear to be difficult to prepare, but this wholesome and unusual dessert is well worth making.

Makes 8

Ingredients

2 cups whole wheat

1 cup chick peas
 (garbanzo beans)

1 cup white kidney beans

½ cup dried apricots

½ cup Turkish figs

¼ cup currants

½ cup raisins

2 cups water

½ cup rice

500 g (1 lb) sugar

½ cup skinless chestnuts (boiled)

2 teaspoons cinnamon

2 cups milk

3 teaspoons rose water

¼ cup pine nuts

½ cup crushed walnuts

½ cup pomegranate seeds

Method

Soak whole wheat overnight. Boil chick peas and kidney beans until tender or use tinned. Soak the apricots, Turkish figs, currants and raisins in warm water for an hour.

In a deep saucepan, boil the whole wheat with 1 cup of water until soft. Add the chick peas, beans, rice and sugar. Boil with the remaining water for 20 minutes. Add the apricots, figs, currants, raisins, chestnuts, pine nuts, cinnamon and milk. Boil 15 minutes more. Remove from the heat and stir in rose water.

Pour into 8 individual serving cups or moulds when it is hot. Leave to cool then refrigerate for 3 hours. Decorate with crushed walnuts and pomegranate seeds.

Baked Kadayif with Mozzarella Cheese

Künefe

Künefe is a very special, crunchy dessert with a cheese filling. Typically we use a special, low-salt regional cheese, but you can use mozzarella as it is very similar. A special copper dish is used to serve künefe and the cooks in kebab restaurants make it in a stone oven. You can buy the kadayif from Turkish and Greek grocery stores and suppliers.

Serves 6

Ingredients

500 g (1 lb) kadayıf
  (shredded dough)
100 g (3½ oz) butter
100 g (3½ oz) sugar
250 g (8 oz) mozzarella cheese
pistachios, for decoration

Syrup
2 cups sugar
3 cups water

Method

Preheat oven to 200°C (400°F/Gas Mark 6).

To make syrup: Place the sugar and water into a saucepan and boil for 25–30 minutes, until it thickens. Leave to cool.

Cut mozzarella into thin slices.

Separate and loosen-up the kadayıf with your hands, and spread into 6 x 12 cm (5 in) oven dishes.

Melt butter then stir in sugar. Spread a little of the butter and sugar mixture over the top of the kadayıf. Place a second layer of kadayıf over the first and spread more butter-sugar mixture on top.

Place the mozzarella evenly over the top, then cover with 2 more layers of kadayıf and butter-sugar mixture.

Bake künefe for 30 minutes until golden brown. Pour warm syrup over hot künefe. Decorate with pistachios and serve hot.

Şekerpare

Special dessert shops in Turkey sell all kinds of syrupy desserts and Şekerpare is one of them. It is a lovely gift to take relatives and friends on bayram (festival day) visits. Şekerpare is my favourite traditional syrupy dessert.

Serves 6

Ingredients

2 eggs
250 g (8 oz) butter
½ cup icing sugar
½ cup semolina
3½ cups plain (all-purpose) flour
2 teaspoon baking powder
2–3 drops vanilla essence
¼ cup pistachio

Syrup

2 cups sugar
3 cups water
juice of ½ lemon

Method

Preheat oven to 180°C (350°F/Gas Mark 4).

To make syrup: Place water and sugar in a saucepan, add lemon juice and boil until the syrup thickens. Leave to cool.

Mix eggs and butter in a mixing bowl until creamy. Beat in icing sugar. Add semolina, flour, baking powder and vanilla essence until combined.

Roll dough out until 2.5 cm (1 in) thick and cut into 1 cm (½ in) long pieces.

Roll the cut pieces into ball shapes and place on a non-stick baking tray. Place a pistachio on top of each ball. Bake for 20–25 minutes.

Pour cold syrup over the sekerpare when still hot. Wait for sekerpare to soak up the syrup. Serve when cool.

Baked Quinces with Cloves

I love this gourmet dessert. Cooked quinces turn dark golden near the seeds.

Makes 6

Ingredients

6 quinces
2 cups sugar
1 teaspoon cloves
1 cup water
double cream

Method

Preheat oven to 180°C (350°F/Gas Mark 4).

Peel the quinces and cut in half, keeping the seeds. Place quinces in an oven dish and sprinkle sugar over the top. Place cloves and quince seeds in the dish. Pour water over the top and bake for 40–50 minutes until quinces are soft and golden.

Serve with double cream when cool.

Kazandibi

Chicken in a dessert you ask? This creative traditional dessert gets its sticky texture from the caramelised chicken and sugar. The smoky taste of this milky dessert is so original and elegant.

Serves 8

Ingredients

1 cup rice
1 x 75 g (3 oz) chicken breast
4 cups milk
1 cup sugar
1½ cups subye (see method)
2 tablespoons rice flour
½ teaspoon salt
cinnamon, for decoration

Method

To make subye: Add ½ cup water to rice in a bowl and leave overnight. Next day, blend with an electric mixer or food processor until rice is dissolved. Strain the mixture through a colander and set aside. (Do not use leftover rice for subye.)

Place chicken breast into a saucepan and pour water over the top to cover. Boil for 30 minutes. Place cooked chicken in cold water in a saucepan to cool then tear into fine strips.

Boil milk in a pan and add chicken strips. Remove from the stove and allow to cool for 30 minutes. Add sugar, salt, subye, rice flour and cook for about 50 minutes, stirring continuously until mixture thickens.

Pour the mixture into a 25 cm x 35 cm (10 in x 14 in) deep baking tray brushed with oil. Burn the bottom surface of the dessert by placing the tray on an iron grill on a stovetop. Leave to cool. Cut in 8 cm (3 in) strips and roll up. Sprinkle with cinnamon for decoration. You can also leave in strips, without rolling, to serve.

Semolina Halva
İrmik Helva

This recipe dates back to the 15th century, from the palace of the Ottoman Empire. In the palace there was a special kitchen dedicated to helva called a Helvahane, where some 800 chefs and staff prepared over 30 different kinds of helva. Helva is prepared at special occasions and celebrations of all kinds. We still make semolina helva on our special days.

Makes 4

Ingredients

½ cup pine nuts
2 cups water
100 g (3½ oz) butter
1½ cups semolina
1½ cups sugar
1 teaspoon cinnamon
extra pine nuts

Method

Roast pine nuts in a pan on low heat and set aside.

Place water in a saucepan and bring to the boil.

Melt butter in a large pan. Add semolina and cook over low heat stirring with a wooden spoon until a medium golden colour. Add pine nuts. Pour boiling water over the semolina and keep stirring over low heat to soak. Mix in sugar well and remove from the heat. Place into 5 cm (2 in) round rings and put them into the refrigerator for an hour.

Remove from ring tin and place on a serving plate. Sprinkle with cinnamon and decorate with pine nuts.

Pistachio Dessert
Katmer

This dessert is often served in kebab shops. If you still have room after a kebab, katmer comes with a juicy syrup to whet your appetite. You can easily prepare it in your kitchen at home.

Makes 4

Ingredients

250 g (8 oz) pistachio nuts
12 sheets filo pastry
100 g (3½ oz) butter
150 g (5 oz) double cream
100 g (3½ oz) sugar

1 teaspoon cooking oil

Syrup
2 cups sugar
3 cups water

Method

Roast pistachios on a baking tray at 150°C (300°F/Gas Mark 2) for 15 minutes then crush with a mortar and pestle.

To make syrup: Place water and sugar in a saucepan and boil over medium heat for about 25 minutes, until the syrup thickens.

Melt butter. Layer three sheets of filo on an oiled baking tray, brushing each sheet well with butter. Spread the double cream over the top of the pastry, sprinkle with sugar and crushed pistachios, then fold pastry in a 20 cm (8 in) envelope shape.

Place cooking oil into a frying pan and cook the pastry on both sides until golden brown.

Place pastry on a serving plate and pour hot syrup over the top. Serve hot.

Muhallebi with Turkish Coffee

This is a very easy and very tasty recipe. As it has a light taste, it can be cooked for after dinner. You can also decorate it with fairy floss.

Serves 4

Ingredients

4 cups milk

4 tablespoons flour

2 tablespoons cornflour (cornstarch)

¾ cup sugar

2 tablespoons butter

2 drop vanilla essence

2 teaspoons Turkish coffee

Ganache

200 g (7 oz) cream

160 g (5½ oz) chocolate

Method

To make ganache: boil cream in a saucepan until you see bubbles, remove from the stove. Add chocolate and whisk until chocolate is melted. Leave to cool.

Boil Turkish coffee with ¼ cup water and 1 teaspoon sugar.

Place milk, flour, cornflour, vanilla and sugar in a pan. Whisk at low heat until muhallebi is thick and starts bubbling. Add butter and remove from the stove. Divide half of the muhallebi and place into your serving glasses. Refrigerate for ten minutes until they are set.

 Add coffee into the other half and stir with whisk on the stove while the mixture is hot. Pour the coffee muhallebi onto the vanilla muhallebi glasses. Place a thin layer of chocolate ganache on each of them.

 Refrigerate at least 2 hours and serve.

Flour Halva

Un Helva

Flour helva is easy to make and I often prepare it when I have a 'dessert crisis'. This helva is one of the most innovative desserts of Turkish cuisine. The ingredients and the outcome is totally unpredictable!

Serves 6

Ingredients

750 ml (1¼ pints) water
100 g (3½ oz) butter
2 cups plain (all-purpose) flour
2 cups sugar
1 teaspoon cinnamon
raspberry sauce (see recipe
 page 99)

Method

In a saucepan, bring water to the boil.

Melt butter in another saucepan. Add flour and stir over medium heat using a wooden spoon until it is a light golden colour. Pour boiling water into the flour and keep stirring to thicken. Remove the pan from the stove, add sugar quickly and mix. Stir in cinnamon.

Using a spoon, take a scoop of the halva and slide onto a serving plate. Serve warm with raspberry sauce and ice-cream.

Sweets

Carrot Truffles
Cezerye

This carrot dessert originated in the Arab peninsula.

A dessert made from carrot may sound strange but these soft and delicious little balls are a tasty, healthy treat. I sometimes dip half of the balls into melted white chocolate for special guests.

Makes 20

Ingredients

3 carrots, peeled
½ cup sugar
1 teaspoon corn syrup
100 g (3½ oz) hazelnut meal
200 g (7 oz) shredded coconut
  plus 2 tablespoons extra

Method

Boil the carrots in a saucepan of water until soft. Puree cooked carrots in a food processor, adding sugar slowly.

Add corn syrup, hazelnut meal and coconut until well combined. The mixture should be like a soft dough. Add more hazelnut meal or coconut if needed. Put in refrigerator until set.

Scoop out rounded tablespoons of dough, roll into balls by hand and roll in extra coconut to serve.

You can decorate these with white chocolate stickes, as pictured. Cut plastic straws in half and fill with melted white chocolate. Place in the refrigerator to set for 20 minutes. Cut the straws to remove the chocolate stick and insert.

Coconut and Almond Balls

Hindistan Cevizli Bademli Toplar

These coloured balls are the yummy treats of wedding dinner tables. They attract a lot of attention because they're so eye-catching. They can be stored in the fridge in a covered container for two weeks.

Makes 20

Ingredients

150 g (5 oz) almond meal

100 g (3½ oz) desiccated coconut

250 g (8 oz) icing sugar

1 teaspoon glucose syrup (or corn syrup)

2 egg whites

1 drop almond essence

food colouring (any colour)

Method

Place almond meal, coconut and icing sugar in a bowl. Add the glucose (corn syrup). Whisk the egg whites then add to the mixture.

Mix gently until you have a non-sticky dough. Add one drop of food colouring and mix in well.

Scoop out spoonfuls of dough and roll into balls by hand. Place on a tray lined with baking paper until set.

Chestnut Drops
Kestane Şekeri

When I learnt that chestnut trees could live for more than a thousand years and they had once been the basic source of flour for southern Europe, my admiration for them grew even more. Chestnut is one of my favourite ingredients to make special desserts, cakes and tarts.I often use them to decorate cakes too. These chestnut delights are easy to prepare, attractive, very tasty and ideal for parties.

Makes 20

Ingredients

500 g (1 lb) fresh chestnuts
  (or chestnut puree)
200 g (7 oz) sugar
200 ml (7 fl oz) water
250 g (8 oz) chocolate

Method

If you can't buy peeled chestnuts, mark an 'X' in the shells and boil for 30 minutes. Let them cool down then peel off the skin. Puree the peeled chestnuts in a food processor then transfer to a large bowl.

Boil the sugar and water in a saucepan for about 25 minutes over medium heat. Pour the syrup into the chestnut puree until you have a soft dough; you may not need all the syrup.

Scoop out spoonfuls of dough and roll into drop shapes by hand. Place in the refrigerator to set for 1 hour, then move to the freezer for 20 minutes.

Melt the chocolate in a bain-marie or microwave.

Dip the chestnut drops into the chocolate using toothpicks. Place on a tray lined with baking paper until the chocolate sets.

Turkish Delight
Lokum

Turkish delight is undoubtedly the most famous Turkish dessert around the world. It has many variations with different ingredients and preparation methods in every region of Turkey.

Makes 25

Ingredients

1 kg (2 lb) sugar

4 cups water

125 g (4 oz) cornflour (cornstarch) plus extra for dusting

1 teaspoon citric acid

100 g (3½ oz) coconut

150 g (5 oz) crushed pistachios

Method

Boil the sugar with $\frac{1}{3}$ of the water until it reaches 130°C (250°F/Gas Mark ½). Using a whisk, mix the cornflour and citric acid with the remaining water. Combine the two mixtures and boil for about 50 minutes over low heat until the mixture thickens. Add the pistachios.

Meanwhile, line a deep 25 cm x 35 cm (10 in x 14 in) baking tray with baking paper and sprinkle with icing sugar and cornflour. Pour the hot mixture into the baking tray. Allow to rest overnight.

The next day, turn the tray upside down onto a surface spread with coconut. Cut lokum into 2 cm x 2 cm (¾ in x ¾ in) cube shapes.

Crunchy Chocolate

Citir Cikolata

I love the combination of crusty and sweet in desserts. This is certainly my choice when it comes to making chocolate as well. I believe the crunchy nuts are the perfect contrast to the unique taste of chocolate.

Serves 20

Ingredients

250 g (8 oz) dark chocolate
150 g (5 oz) pistachio
100 g (3½ oz) cornflakes
50 g (2 oz) raisins

Method

Melt chocolate in a bain-marie or microwave. Remove from the heat.

Roast pistachios on a baking tray for 15 minutes at 150°C (300°F/Gas Mark 2). Leave to cool.

Mix all the ingredients into the melted chocolate. Place large spoonfuls of chocolate mix onto a baking tray lined with baking paper.

Allow to cool in refrigerator for 10 minutes. Store in an airtight jar at room temperature.

Fried Cinnamon Dough Balls

Lokma

Doughnuts are the favorite fried dough everywhere around the world. They are also widely welcomed in Turkey. Even famous cafes dedicate a corner to these hot, golden, crusty and sweet balls. The shape is ball like and the taste is very sweet. So unlike soft American donuts, crunchy Turkish lokma are served with water.

Serves 8

Ingredients

2 cups plain (all-purpose) flour
1 teaspoon dry yeast
2 teaspoons sugar
1 egg
2 cups water
2 cups cooking oil
1 teaspoon cinnamon

Syrup
2½ cups sugar
2½ cups water

Method

To make the syrup: Place sugar and water in a saucepan and boil for 20 minutes until the syrup thickens.

To make the lokma: Place flour in a mixing bowl and make a well in the centre. Place yeast and sugar in the well. Pour in water as you mix with a spatula. The dough should be runny, so do not put in extra flour.

Heat cooking oil in a frying pan until hot. Oil your palm and scoop out dough, rolling and squeezing into tight balls.

Place the balls into the heated oil with a tablespoon. Cook the lokma until they are a bright golden colour.

Place in a large, deep dish and poor cooled syrup over the top.

Allow to cool and sprinkle with cinnamon. Serve when still warm but not too hot.

Pistachio Brittle

Krokan

Crunchy pistachio brittle is often sold in boxes in Turkey. It is widely loved around the country and it isn't difficult to finish the box. Some of them are prepared with sugar caramel whereas others are prepared with both chocolate and caramel. I have given the original recipe here but you may want to eat it dipped into a milky chocolate.

Serves 8

Ingredients

250 g (8 oz) pistachios
300 g (10 oz) sugar
50 ml (1½ fl oz) water
1 tablespoon oil

Method

Roast pistachios on a baking tray at 150°C (300°F/Gas Mark 2) for 15 minutes.

Place sugar and water into a saucepan and bring to boil until thickened and golden. Stir in oil.

Mix pistachios into syrup quickly using a wooden spatula. Spread krokan quickly and carefully onto an oiled baking tray. Leave to cool then break into pieces.

Drinks

Puerperal Sherbet

Şerbet

Sherbets are the juices of boiled fruits and herbs. Sherbet making is a living tradition handed down by the Ottomans. Different sherbets are made in the various regions of Turkey. Some are spicy and some taste only of the boiled fruits. These creative boiled juices were the herbal healers of their time. Below is a recipe from the southern regions of Turkey, which heals and empowers mothers after they give birth.

Serves 6

Ingredients

2 L (4 pints) water

2 cinnamon sticks

10 black pepper seeds

10 cloves seeds

1 whole ginger

1 whole galangal root (available from Asian grocery stores)

1 whole nutmeg

2 cups sugar

ground walnuts, for garnish

Method

Put the water in a large saucepan and bring to the boil. Add all ingredients except the sugar and allow to boil down until 1.5 L (3 pints) of liquid remains. Add sugar. Keep boiling until 1 L (2 pints) of the sherbet remains.

Serve hot, sprinkled with ground walnut.

Turkish Coffee

World-famous Turkish coffee is an Arabic coffee prepared by boiling finely powdered roast coffee beans in a special pot (cezve), sometimes with sugar. It is served in a cup and drunk after the dregs settle. It is common throughout the Middle East, North Africa, Caucasus and the Balkans, and in expatriate communities and restaurants in the rest of the world. A Turkish saying that shows the importance of coffee in Turkish culture is: 'One cup of coffee will be remembered for 40 years.'

You can buy Turkish coffee from gourmet supermarkets. To prepare it you need a narrow-topped small boiling pot called a cezve, a teaspoon and a heating apparatus. The best coffee is done in coal ashes or in a tray of fine sand heated from the bottom. Turkish coffee is served in a demitasse (fincan) cup. Some modern cups do have handles, but traditional cups did not; coffee was drunk either by handling the cup with the fingertips or, more often, by placing the cup in a zarf, a metal container with a handle.

Makes 2

Ingredients

4 teaspoons Turkish coffee
2 teaspoons sugar
2 Turkish coffee cups of water

Method

As with other ways of preparing coffee, the best Turkish coffee is made from freshly roasted beans ground just before brewing. A dark roast is preferable but even a medium roast coffee will yield a strong aroma and taste. The grinding is done either by pounding in a mortar (the original method) or using a mill (the more usual method today), and the end result is a fine coffee powder. Beans for Turkish coffee are ground into a powder that is even finer than the powder made by pump-driven espresso makers.

Add all the ingredients to the cezve and stir over low heat. Transfer half into the Turkish coffee cups after the coffee comes to boil. Continue stirring the remaining coffee until it boils and transfer the rest to the cups with as much foam as you can.

Turkish Tea

Turkish people are the second largest consumers of black tea after the British. Turkey is also one of the largest tea-growing countries thanks to the climate on the north coast on the edge of the Black Sea.

Tea is almost like a substitute for water in Turkey and it is the first drink offered to guests, even at workplaces and business meetings. It is the social, official and casual drink for Turkish people. Variations of Turkish tea can be easily found all over the world at Turkish and Middle Eastern stores.

My favourite is black tea with a bergamot aroma, commonly known as Earl Grey. The recipe below is for spice and flavour lovers.

Serves 2

Ingredients

2 teaspoons Turkish black tea
1 slice bergamot or lime
1 teaspoon cloves
6 cups water

Method

To make Turkish tea you need two separate pots for the water and the tea mixture, which sit on top of each other. Place the water in the bottom pot, and place all the ingredients in the other pot on top. Bring the water to the boil then transfer half of the boiling water to the tea mixture pot and continue boiling the water at a low heat. Allow to boil until all the floating tea sinks to the bottom in the top pot.

Strain the tea mixture into thin Turkish tea glasses, filling one third of the glass. Add boiling water to fill the glass. Serve hot.

Boza

Thick, creamy boza is a popular fermented beverage in Turkey. It is a malt drink made from maize (corn) and fermented wheat. It has a thick consistency and a low alcohol content, usually around one per cent, and has a slightly acidic sweet flavour. Boza is served with cinnamon and roasted chickpeas and is consumed mainly in the winter months. The Ottoman Empire was known to feed its army with boza as it is rich in carbohydrates and vitamins. This recipe requires preparation a few days beforehand.

Makes 12

Ingredients

2 cups bulghur (cracked dry wheat)

20 cups water

½ cup sugar + 2½ tablespoons sugar extra

2 tablespoons flour

½ teaspoon dry yeast

2 teaspoons cinnamon

½ cup yogurt

½ tablespoon vanilla extract

Method

Place the bulghur and 11 cups of water in a big bowl and let it rest overnight at room temperature, covered with a tea towel.

The next day, add ½ cup sugar to the bowl, transfer to a large saucepan and cook over low heat for 2 hours. Let cool and blend the mix using a hand blender. Pour through a colander, keeping the remaining wheat. Transfer the liquid to a bowl or jug and refrigerate.

In a saucepan, add the wheat and 8 cups of water and cook over a low heat for 45 minutes. Drain and transfer the wheat mix to the refrigerator as well.

Place the flour in a deep saucepan and add 2/3 cup of water and cook, stirring with a wooden spoon, until thickened. Remove from the stove and add 2 teaspoons sugar. Stir until the sugar dissolves. Allow to cool and add the yogurt.

Dissolve the yeast in ¼ cup of water and allow to rest for 5 minutes. Add the yeast to the flour and yoghurt mix. Allow to rest 30 minutes at room temperature. Add the yeast mixture to the drained wheat and add vanilla and 2½ tablespoons of sugar and allow to rest for two days.

Stir well before serving. Serve with roasted chickpeas and sprinkle with cinnamon.

Salep

A popular winter drink to warm you up, the powder called salep or sahlep, is made from the roots of a wild orchid that only grows in Anatolia. It has a very pleasant taste and is believed to have healing qualities. Salep is also widely used for the preparation of a gourmet ice-cream giving it a unique flavour. You can find this expensive spice at selected spice shops.

Serves 4

Ingredients

2 teaspoons salep (from gourmet grocers)
200 g (7 oz) sugar
500 ml (18 fl oz) water
500 ml (18 fl oz) milk
ground cinnamon, to serve

Method

Mix salep and sugar in water and bring to the boil. Heat the milk to boiling in another saucepan. As the salep mixture thickens, add the boiling milk.

Sprinkle cinnamon on top before serving. Serve hot.

Glossary

Poğaça is a dough based savory pastry. The name comes from Italian foccaccia as they have a close pronunciation. Likewise, çörek is a generic name used for both sweet and savory pastries.

Simit is a very popular ring-shaped bread sold in the streets of Turkey. It comes in different kinds and flavours. It is a common sight to see a young man carrying a big timber tray full of simits on his head, announcing his presence with a chant as he walks through the streets.

Yufka is thin phyllo dough rolled out in a big circle and cooked briefly over a large hot dome-shaped metal surface. It is a basic ingredient in many different recipes. It can be found in shops and delis which sell Turkish food.

Gözleme is a food typical of rural areas, made of thin lavash bread or phyllo dough folded around a variety of fillings such as spinach, cheese and parsley, minced meat or potatoes and cooked on a large griddle (traditionally called sac, it looks like an inverted wok). Gözleme has become very popular in Australia and nowadays can be found, sold freshly cooked, at many markets, suburban fetes and carnivals.

Ayran is a popular Turkish drink. Usually a one-to-one mixture of yogurt and water, shaken with some salt and served cold, it is a very refreshing and healthy beverage especially on hot summer days. It goes really well with fresh gözleme or börek.

Katmer is another traditional rolled out dough. It comes in different regional varieties and can be salty or sweet depending on the filling.

Çörek otu is commonly sprinkled on top of many pastries and breads to add a spicy taste. The scientific name is Nigella, also known as Black Cumin or Black Sesame.

Mahlep or mahaleb is one of the lesser known secrets of the Turkish bakers as it adds a very pleasant aroma to pastries, especially special types of simit. It translates as mahaleb, mahaleb cherry or St. Lucie's cherry. It is sold in powder form.

Börek is the general name for savory pastries made with yufka (phyllo dough), which consists of many thin layers of dough. The use of layered dough goes back to the nomadic lifestyle of early Central Asian Turks. The combination of domed metal sac (which is like an inverted wok) and oklava (the Turkish rod-style rolling pin) enabled the invention of the layered dough style used in börek (especially in su böreği, or 'water pastry', a savory pastry with cheese filling), and desserts such as güllaç and baklava.

Çiğ börek (also known as Tatar böreği) is stuffed with minced meat and fried. Kol böreği is another well-known version that takes its name from its shape (kol means 'arm'), as do fincan (coffee cup), muska (talisman), Gül böreği (rose) or Sigara böreği (cigarette). Other traditional Turkish böreks include Talaş böreği (phyllo dough filled with vegetables and diced meat) and, Puf böreği. Laz böreği is a sweet type of börek, widespread in the Black Sea region.

Pide is probably the most popular Turkish style bread. Plain pide has come to be known in Australia as Turkish bread. The ones that come with toppings are commonly referred to as Turkish pizza. Lahmacun is an Arab inspired version of pide with a spicy mince topping.

Homemade cookies are commonly called kurabiye in Turkish. The most common types are acıbadem kurabiyesi (prepared only with egg, sugar and almond), un kurabiyesi (flour kurabiye) and cevizli kurabiye (kurabiye with walnut). Another dough based dessert is ay çöreği.

Tahin-pekmez is a traditional combination especially in rural areas. Tahin is sesame paste (tahini) and pekmez is grape molasses. These are sold separately and mixed to taste before consumption. Highly nutritious and energising to start the day, just mix one-to-one and have on toast!

Among milk-based desserts, the most popular ones are muhallebi, sütlaç (rice pudding), keşkül, kazandibi (meaning the bottom of 'kazan' (cauldron) because of its burnt surface), and tavuk göğsü (a sweet, gelatinous, milk pudding dessert quite similar to kazandibi, to which very thinly peeled chicken breast is added to give a subtle chewy texture).

Going by the popular adage 'Let's eat sweet and talk sweet' Turks love a sugar hit in the form of a syrupy dessert after a big meal.

Kadaif (Kadayıf) is a common Turkish dessert made with finely shredded yufka. There are different types of kadaif: tel (wire) or burma (wrung) kadayıf, both of which can be prepared with either walnut or pistachio fillings. Künefe contains wire kadayıf with a layer of melted cheese in between and it is served hot with pistachio or walnut.

One of the world-renowned desserts of Turkish cuisine is baklava. Baklava can have cream, pistachio or walnut fillings. Turkish cuisine has a range of baklava-like desserts which include şöbiyet, bülbül yuvası ('nightingale's nest'), saray sarması, sütlü nuriye, and sarı burma. The well-known version of baklava in this country is the Arabian style, which a Turk would call 'dry' baklava. A good Turkish baklava is syrupy, yet still has crusty top layers, well-baked crunchy bottom layers and a delightful soft middle layer. It is an absolute delight and the best way to polish off a big meal with some Turkish coffee or tea.

Other popular desserts include; Revani (with semolina and starch), şekerpare, kalburabasma, dilber dudağı (sweetheart's lips), vezir parmağı (vizier's finger), hanım göbeği (lady's belly-button), kemalpaşa (named after the Turkish national leader, Mustafa Kemal Atatürk), tulumba, zerde, höşmerim, paluze, irmik tatlısı/peltesi, lokma. You will find many of these delightful desserts in the book.

Lokum (Turkish delight), which was eaten for digestion after meals and called 'rahat hulkum' in the Ottoman era, is another well-known sweet/candy with a range of varieties.

Helva (halva): un helvası (flour halva), irmik helvası (cooked with semolina and pine nuts). Helva, as it is known and sold here in both Greek and Turkish versions, is the tahini version.

Aşure can be described as a sweet soup containing boiled beans, wheat and dried fruits. Sometimes cinnamon and rose water are added when being served. According to legend, it was first cooked on Noah's Ark and contained seven different ingredients in one dish. The Anatolian peoples have cooked and are still cooking aşure, especially during the month of Muharrem.

Some traditional Turkish desserts are fruit-based: ayva tatlısı (quince), incir tatlısı (fig), kabak tatlısı (pumpkin), elma tatlısı (apple) and armut tatlısı (pear). Fruit is cooked in a pot or in the oven with sugar, cloves and cinnamon (without adding water). After being chilled, they are served with walnut or pistachio and cream.

Cezerye is a kind of 'carrot truffle', a sweet treat made with carrots, nuts and herbs.

Boza is a traditional tangy, fermented maize drink, it could possibly be an ancestor of beer...Light alcohol content of about 1 per cent.

Salep or sahlep is a drink made from the dried and powdered roots of a wild orchid. The name comes from an Arabic term meaning 'fox testicles' and was believed to have aphrodisiac effects. It is a popular drink especially in winter and is believed to relieve cold and flu symptoms.

Recipe Index

First published in Australia in 2010 by

New Holland Publishers (Australia) Pty Ltd

Sydney * Auckland * London * Cape Town

1/66 Gibbes Street Chatswood NSW 2067 Australia * 218 Lake Road Northcoate Auckland New Zealand
New Edgeware Road London W2 2EA United Kingdom * 80 McKenzie Street Cape Town 8001 South Africa

National Library of Australia Cataloguing-in-Publication entry:

Akcakanat, Deniz.

Turkish bakery delight / Deniz Akcakanat.

9781741109252 (hbk.)

Desserts--Turkey.

Confectionery--Turkey.

Cookery, Turkish.

641.8609561

Publishers: Linda Williams

Publishing Manager: Lliane Clarke

Project Editor: Diane Jardine

Editor: Jenny Scepanovic

Designer: Amanda Tarlau

Production Manager: Olga Dementiev

Printer: Toppan Leefung Printers Limited

Photography: Evren Arısoy, Ekim Altunigne